POCKET GUIDE TO
NUMEROLOGY

ALAN OKEN

The Crossing Press
Freedom, California

To Eric and Julie Oken, with love and blessings

With sincere appreciation to my assistant, apprentice, and dear friend, Vance Lesauskis, whose dedicated work and support aided greatly in the writing of this book.

Copyright © 1996 by Alan Oken

Cover illustration and design by Tara Eoff
Text design by Sheryl Karas
Printed in the U.S.A.

For information on bulk purchases or group discounts for
this and other Crossing Press titles, please contact our
Special Sales Manager at 800-777-1048.

ISBN 0-89594-826-5

CONTENTS

Introduction...5

1: What Is Numerology?....................................6

2: The Numbers—Numerology's
Basic Principles..8

3: Your Destiny Number................................25

4: Your Personal Year Number.....................48

5: Your Success Year Number.......................58

6: The Numbers in Your Name.....................65

7: Your Personality Number..........................86

8: Your Soul Urge Number..........................106

Conclusion: It All Adds Up!........................125

Introduction

Each of us is intimately interwoven into the infinite fabric of the Universe. But how can we come to know that our own little life is united within the One Great Life of Creation? What kind of helpful tools can we use to extend our vision? How can we learn to see farther, wider, and more deeply into ourselves and our connection to the Cosmos?

Seers and sages throughout human history have had profound vision and insight. In their pursuit of the meaning of life and in their urge to help others, they have been the inventors of the knowledge we need to see ourselves as more than just reflections in our bathroom mirror. Three of these helpful inventions are astrology, the tarot cards, and numerology, valuable ways of knowing about life and ourselves. Perhaps the easiest for us to use and understand is numerology.

As you study the pages of this book, you will find a much larger world unfolding to your eyes, mind, and heart. You will come in contact with your own particular Destiny Path based on the numbers of your date of birth. From the letters of your name, you will see a clear portrait emerging of your character, your personality, and the nature of your relationships. Perhaps most important of all, your adventure in numerology can bring you a wonderful awareness of your innermost life purpose—the urge of your Soul.

The *Pocket Guide to Numerology* gives several simple methods of finding the hidden meanings contained within your name and birthday, and all you have to do is add. You may also wish to apply what you know to the birth dates and names of the people closest to you, and to share what you have discovered with your friends and loved ones, bringing your gift of numerology to them.

What is Numerology?

Numerology is the occult and metaphysical science of numbers. It is the path of understanding that gives depth and meaning to the simple digits represented by our ten fingers and toes. As a result of our appreciation and grasp of numerology, we know that we are connected in the deepest sense to all that is and everything that will be in the Cosmos. That's quite a remarkable gift for simply being able to count from one to ten!

Numerology is to traditional mathematics what psychology is to anatomy. Mathematics, like anatomy, speaks about our physical universe, its nature, structure, dimensions, and purpose. Numerology and psychology address the less tangible aspects of existence. Just as psychology teaches us about the inner motivations behind our actions, activities, instincts, and responses to life, so too does numerology speak about the hidden world contained within the simplest of numbers. Our job is to unlock these mysteries so that our lives are led with a *meaning* known to us. Once we are in touch with this meaning—this real purpose for why we are on Earth—we can then proceed to create lives that truly fulfill and enrich us.

What is known to us as the modern science of numerology has is origins in ancient times. Numerology was formulated by a Greek scholar and mystic named Pythagoras. About 2,600 years ago, in 581 B.C., when Pythagoras was just a boy of sixteen, he left his home to study and expand his understanding of life. He sailed forth from his native island of Samos and went to schools in

Phoenicia, Babylon, and Egypt. He returned home in 545 B.C., and he founded his own university. But his most important work was accomplished in the then-Greek colony of Croatia, in southern Italy, where a branch of his university took root and provided education in philosophy, music, mathematics, culture, and metaphysics. During this period, he also created the science of numerology. It is this work upon which all subsequent numerology is based.

The best way to profit from reading the *Pocket Guide to Numerology* is to work with it. First make sure that you are familiar with the basics: the significance of Numbers One through Nine, plus Zero and the two so-called "Master Numbers" of Eleven and Twenty-Two. This will all be discussed in Chapter 2. Each of the other chapters of this book (3 through 8) begins with a simple formula to help you discover more about your destiny, character, and the best years of your life for accomplishing your goals and projects. You will enjoy experimenting and working with your own name and birthday numbers and will find many insights applying what you know to other people in your life.

I am sure that you will find your adventure with numerology to be exciting and uplifting. Should you wish to continue expanding your numerological awareness, a reference and resource guide is provided at the end of the book.

Welcome to the mystery of numbers. After reading and working just a little bit with this book, you will find that this myself reveals itself to you, and the beauty and excitement of your life will increase.

7	6	6	4		3	3	3	2
G	O	O	D		L	U	C	K

The Numbers—
Numerology's Basic
Principles

You are about to begin a journey of self-discovery through the numbers. In order to do this, you will need a clear and precise understanding of numerology's "alphabet." Unlike the English language, which has twenty-six letters, numerology requires you to know only twelve. These are the Numbers One through Nine, plus Eleven, Twenty-Two, and Zero. Once you have a mastery of this important dozen, your Destiny opportunity, Personality factors, Soul Urge, and Personal and Success Years will unfold their secrets to you.

The following numbers and their meanings represent some of the most important principles of life. This chapter presents these twelve numbers as integral parts of the great Cycle of Life. Each number is one facet of a universal whole of which each of us is a part. As you study the following pages, recognize that each of the numbers is a stage in the unfolding of the One Life Force. You are part of that One, and your own particular numbers will tell you a great deal about where in the cycle of the numbers you belong. First, look at the numbers and their descriptions from an objective point of view. Learn the basic principles involved and the numerological keywords. Chapters 3 through 8 will make the numbers increasingly more specific to your life. You will then come to see how these twelve simple numbers can intimately affect you and the people closest to you.

Your journey begins with the Number One.

NUMBER ONE

As the first number, Number One is the number of beginnings. It represents initiation and the initial cause of things. Number One gives drive, inspiration, and the motivation to live and experience life. Number One is the most projective and outgoing of all the numbers. It is through Number One that an idea or a person is born into the world. One is a separate individual, always at work becoming more of itself. As an individual, each person has his or her own particular point of view and modes of self-expression. In this respect, Number One seems to be saying: "I am myself and I want, I need, and I desire to be me."

During the Number One stage of the great Life Cycle, individuals learn how to express their own abilities. They move through life with a deep connection to the need to experience their own mistakes and start up again, overcoming personal limitations through their immediate confrontations with life. As a child grows, his need to expand his influence on his environment also grows. He requires a more efficient means of locomotion in order to dominate the surroundings. Number One falls down many times but always picks himself up again and again until he masters the art of walking (and then watch him run!). Number One is therefore the symbol of personal drive. A strong personal drive, a strong will power, keeps a person moving through all of life's obstacles. A weakness of will and drive leads to repeated failures and the acceptance of obstacles as the reality of life. Number One teaches the lessons of the right use of will and power.

A pure Number One type of person is very identified with himself. When immature, he tends to strike out into life without regard for people and the other social circumstances in his environment. Once a Number One has a more developed personality, we then find a person who is a pioneer, opening the way for others as he overcomes his own personal battles one at a time. It isn't until we reach the Number Two stage of life that we realize that we must revolve around the center of the Universe and not try to force everything and everyone to revolve around ourselves.

Even though Number One represents a very egocentric nature, this is a vitally important stage for each person's growth and development. In order to expand, we first must be aware of our center. Number One strongly emphasizes those individuals who are leaders. They are the prime motivators and initiators of actions and activities, and they work to create evolutionary changes for humanity and the planet.

Keywords: independent, individualistic, martial, original, assertive, dominating, forceful, willful

NUMBER TWO

Out of the One comes the Many. Two is the number of duality, indicating relationship and what is called the "Law of Opposites." Thus it is through Number Two that we express the relationship between such things as left and right, up and down, cold and hot, dark and light, even male and female.

Number Two brings about a sense of separation, yet at the same time, this separation awakens within us the need to bring things together. We could also say that Number Two is the "urge to merge." There is a very old saying, "Opposites attract." So the Number Two carries a strong magnetic, attractive appeal. People who have the Number Two as a prominent part of their numerological make-up are learning how to interact with others. They are project-ing their individuality (1) but are also becoming increasing-ly more receptive to how other people express themselves. When Number Two is a powerful influence in someone's life, that person has a deep sense of connection with people and the planet, and can easily cooperate with both.

This sense of receptivity and sensibility to others in no way interferes with or challenges the Number Two's sense of herself. But if the Number Two is absent or weak within a person's numerological framework (see Chapters 3 through 8), he or she will have a hard time working in coop-erative life situations. These individuals tend to live in an ivory tower of their own thoughts and desires, not taking into consideration other people's feelings or the ecological needs of their environment. They are thus stagnating at the Number One stage of development.

When you create a relationship between the musical notes of the scale, you get chords. When you further this relationship through the addition of rhythm, you get music. When you move consciously into the Number Two stage of development, you begin to move to the music of life. You are then adapting to the rhythms, to the ebbs and flows of life on our planet. At the Number Two stage of the great cycle, you are becoming receptive to the sounds of life around you, as well as to your relationship to them. Number Two is cooperating in such a way as to increase the harmony of all these relationships. If Number Two has developed her personal identity (1) enough to feel secure, then she can dance along in harmony and even contribute to the beauty of the music.

Keywords: adaptable, understanding, gentle, cooperative, receptive, cautious

NUMBER THREE

Number One teaches us how to project our individuality into the various experiences of life. Number Two expands upon this sense of self and teaches us how to create relationships with the people, ideas, and objects in our environment. When we come to Number Three, we are involved in the development of an active intelligence, use of information, and creation of our communication skills. It is also through the Number Three that we learn to organize our lives intelligently so that we may build the necessary foundations (4) to expand our life potentials (5).

Number Three represents the time when we are in school learning how to use words, numbers, and tools that allow us to externalize our inner potentials. In this respect, Number Three rules such things as musical instruments, computers, pens and paper, calculators, paintbrushes, etc. It is through the Number Three that we learn how to structure a sentence to organize ideas. It also gives us the names for the notes, the particular types of rhythms, and the kinds of tones expressed in the lyrics and sounds.

The odd numbers are all projective by nature, and Number Three is concerned with the expression and circulation of information. Composing, writing, journalism, and the media are all under the influence of this number. People strongly connected to Number Three are always talking and verbally expressing themselves. They like to move their ideas out into the world. These are usually sociable and friendly people. They are intelligent, with a keen sense of mind and reason. When the Number Three is a weak influence in a person's life, he tends to be quiet and withdrawn, unable to clearly communicate what he feels and thinks.

Keywords: intelligent, communicative, sociable, learned, creative, diversified, dramatic, expressive

NUMBER FOUR

We all seek to be creative. As human beings, the major vehicle of our creativity is our minds. Often, we receive a bolt of inspiration (1) which awakens us to our possibilities. We look around and see how we can relate (2) what we see inside our minds to the rest of the world. Finally, we examine our particular talents and abilities (3) to see how we can express our ideas tangibly. In essence, Number Four represents the practical, physical world of the many forms life may take. Four is the number of Mother Earth. She is composed of four elements (earth, water, air, and fire) and moves through four seasons. The first three numbers symbolize qualities that we develop inside ourselves. Number Four takes these qualities and uses them to create what is solid and tangible outside of us.

The science of numerology uses numbers as symbols. Everything in the outer, objective world can be said to be a symbol of an inner quality of our lives. For example, when we want to experience movement (1), we create the idea of travel (3). We then can come up with a form (4) for the kind of travel we wish to do, such as an automobile or an airplane. In this we have the action of $1 + 3 = 4$!

Number Four is about day-to-day life. It speaks to us about the structure of society. It is more concerned with what is permanent than with what is transient, more involved with what is solid than with what may vanish into thin air. Number Four represents foundation and tradition, and in this respect, Number Four can be said to be quite conservative. It is after we graduate from school (3) that we go out into the world and make something solid and permanent with our lives.

Perhaps at the outset of this stage of our development we don't make a particularly strong impact because we are still learning how the patterns of life (3) work. Older, more solidified people (4) look at younger people and see their potential (1). We have to go through a period of training in relating (2) who we are to what we do. We are at the stage of learning how to use our tools (3) so that we may apply them to our daily life in practical ways (4). As we grow, we become increasingly involved with the social structures that surround us (4). Without our own foundations, without the solid structuring of our connection with social life, we will not be able to expand our potential for further growth and benefit both ourselves and others. Once we are grounded, we can move into the expansive stage of Number Five.

Keywords: stability, firmness, security, conservative, practical, forms, systems, solidity, objectivity

NUMBER FIVE

Placed midway between the prime numbers One and Nine, Number Five indicates a turning point and major life decision. At this point of a person's development, one asks the question: "Have I learned well enough the basic qualities of life, as symbolized by the Numbers One through Four, so that I may move into those powerful, mystical, and creatively productive realms in Numbers Six through Nine?"

Have I developed enough personal power (1) to be able to withstand the pressure of moving into the world of unknown challenges and experiences without losing myself?

Am I receptive enough (2) to recognize and merge (2) with such experiences so that I may come to know a new way of living? Do I have enough tools (3) to develop my own ideas about these new circumstances? And do I have the proper connection to the world around me (4) so that I may have a positive effect on the planet and the lives of others (4)?

Number Five indicates the stage in life when a person breaks free from his solidified patterns of behavior (4) and searches for new ways of living. Five stimulates the conservative, stable, and solidified nature of Number Four into experiences and forms that are expanding, evolving, and growing. Five is when an individual takes the step that will lead him beyond his present sense of personal limitations and confining social structures.

It is through Number Five that people discover those new life situations that awaken new qualities and greater potentials within themselves. Five is the adventurer in search of other lands or the mystic seeking an expansion of consciousness. The Number Five person is curious, active, and ready to try anything. She is the visionary who has a glimpse of what awaits her as she puts her right foot forward. Five is able and resourceful. She avoids becoming entrapped as she searches for a greater sense of personal freedom. A person lacking in these characteristics would be much more content to let the days pass without this search for a more expansive life.

Keywords: expansion, change, adventure, speculation, visions, growing, evolution, curious, active, resourceful

NUMBER SIX

Number Six takes a person to a stage in life in which he can bring into the world the expanded visions obtained through Number Five. The goal is to find a receptive place (2) in society (4) for all of his realizations and creative potential (2+4 = 6). He does this through integrating himself more firmly into his surroundings. He has obtained a sense of responsibility and structure (4) and has added to his life potential (5).

Number Six is a double three. Thus a person can use the tools and skills (3) he has mastered and creatively design ways of communicating his particular talents to a larger audience (3+3 = 6). This element of communication is typical of Number Six. Six is also a very artistic life expression. It is a number of harmony and balance, seeking to bring its unique sense of beauty into the environment.

This urge for harmony not only extends outward into society at large; it is a fundamental subjective urge that finds its initial expression in the family. Six is thus the number of domestic wholeness and family unity. People who are strongly influenced by the Number Six are very aware of the people in their immediate surroundings. Friendships are extremely important, and the need for right human relationships in every area of life is paramount. The Number Six demonstrates the desire for close companionship, intimate partnership, group harmony, and a stable emotional life.

Six teaches us to communicate with compassion and understanding. It has long passed the Number One stage in which a more forceful and assertive self-expression is necessary. Six brings us the awareness of people's and society's ills and limitations. Those of us with a Six as our Destiny or

Name Number will find that we are very much geared to serving others and to maintaining a healthy environment for everyone's benefit. Six gives the ability to bring those ideas into the world that can make it a better place for the entire human family.

Keywords: harmony, creativity, justice, balance, love, compassion, service, art, symbols

NUMBER SEVEN

We could call the Number Seven the "Philosopher's Number," as it is the prime component in so many mystical and occult formulas. In effect, the Number Seven is a number of cycles and of created wholeness. Astrologers take the number of signs in the zodiac (12) and multiply them by 7 to get the natural life span of a human being (84 years). There are also seven power centers in the human energy field (or "aura") known as "chakras," which correspond to the seven major endocrine glands in the human body. The Bible tells of the "Seven Thrones Before God" and the "Seven Days of Creation."

After all of the Divinity's work to create the world, and our own work to co-create our little lives, it is on the seventh day of the week that we rest. Thus it is through the Number Seven that we become introspective and pull inside for repose, contemplation, and understanding. Seven is neither a worldly nor a materialistic number. Many people strongly influenced by its vibrations tend to be rather mental in orientation. They like the fields of science and enjoy working in laboratories doing research. Number Seven often produces loners, individuals who are very much connected to their own deep inner processes of investigation. In this respect, Seven is definitely not the socially oriented Six.

Seven also produces a very strong spiritual nature. It is only a leap in consciousness up from the mental to the intuitive level of being that separates the physical from the metaphysical, astronomy from astrology, geometry from geomancy, and psychology from psychism. Seven influences people on these more ethereal and occult paths. The beauty created in the world of the arts through the Number Six takes on a more mental and abstract shape through the Number Seven. This works to create "thought-forms" and gives rise to all sorts of philosophical and scientific speculation, investigation, and discovery.

Keywords: philosophical, analytical, quiet, introspective, understanding, intuitive, inspirational, reclusive

NUMBER EIGHT

After the metaphysical and scientific experimentation contained in the activities of the Number Seven, Eight brings us back to earth with some solid practicality. Eight is, after all, double four (4+4 = 8). Eight takes those lessons of structure and responsibility learned through the earlier numerological expressions and develops them further to affect our practical life. It is through the Eight that we build businesses, enterprises, and empires!

Let's take the invention of the automobile from stages One through Eight to see how things unfold according to numerological symbology. It is obvious that almost everything and everyone has the inner urge for movement and growth (1). This need to get around has a lot to do with creating primary relationships in response to our desires and actions (2). What is then created is the idea of travel (3) and the necessity to obtain those tools and vehicles to help us get around. Awakening to this need, an inventor begins to develop the structure of engines, spark plugs, accelerators, etc. (4). Co-workers envision the whole of society moving more efficiently if automobile travel is made accessible to everyone (5). These visions are expanded into pictures of entire families and societies communicating and traveling together (6). We now have expanded from the simple automobile seating two or four people to buses, trams, and trolleys. Sociologists and travel experts enter the scene and outline plans and projects to use these new inventions for even greater social benefit (7). Financial backers are attracted to the commercial possibilities of such methods of transportation. They build factories, hiring many men and women to do the work, creating new towns and cities (8).

Number Eight allows for the assumption of power along with responsibility. Eight carries within its vibration a high degree of ambition and a strong sense of force that is extended to all creative projects. People strongly affected by the Number Eight are good at selling their products and reaping the resulting financial rewards for the risks they have taken. In effect, Number Eight is about material satisfaction. Eight works to fulfill the needs of our material life in order to satisfy the vision of how life may be better lived on Earth.

Keywords: ambition, power, production, money, security, practicality, materialism

NUMBER NINE

Nine is the number of completion. A circle represents the feeling of unity symbolized by Nine, as it contains 360 degrees (3+6+0 = 9). With Number Nine, the primary number cycle reaches its conclusion. Nine is thus filled with life's experiences.

Number Nine carries the qualities of compassion, understanding, and selflessness. People who are strongly affected by the Number Nine in terms of their Destiny, Name, Personality, or Soul Urge Numbers usually express generosity, benevolence, and patience. They are involved with other people's welfare, helping them to grow through the sharing of their deeper perception into life's meanings. The experience of Nine is one of integration and synthesis, inclusivity, and universality. Nine is the link we have with the rhythmic ebb and flow of life. It teaches us to return what we have been given so that the creative energy that passes through us may continue to circulate.

Nine brings freedom. When we are free from obsessive personal desires, we are liberated into the world of Nine. We can then find great joy in giving. Part of that joy is in letting others give to us. This giving and sharing, releasing and receiving, serves to expand our consciousness and bring more love into the world.

Mahatma Gandhi, for example, had a Nine Destiny Number and lived out the qualities of the Nine as his Life Path. His strong and forceful presence of love created enormous changes in India. He served his people by trying to instill the concept of social unity in order to help them move beyond ethnic divisions as well as create freedom from colonial oppression.

Keywords: completion, selflessness, compassion, generosity, benevolence, patience, endings

ZERO

We now know that numbers can represent the qualities and characteristics of expressions of energy. This energy we call Life. But Zero is not a true number. Zero is the "all and everything," the alpha and the omega. It is in essence the total potential of the expression of the Life Force. We could say that Zero represents the unity and creative totality of Divinity. Zero is symbolic of Spirit. Unlike the numbers which stand for energy patterns, types of people, objects, stages in the development of ideas, etc., Zero is none of these. Zero is the *potential* of creativity.

When an individual (1) merges with Spirit (0), he or she moves to the next "octave" of life (1+0 = 10). Embodying potential powers, sensibilities, and abilities that are beyond the scope of most people, these individuals are endowed with a special "karma," a special destiny, that can affect the lives of many. At the very least, they are experiencing a lifetime of special significance for their own personal development. Numerology expresses this state of having merged with the Zero through the two "Master Numbers," 11 and 22.

THE MASTER NUMBERS

When 11 or 22 appears as a person's Destiny, Name, Personality, or Soul Urge Number, a potential exists in that individual's life for a greater degree of awareness than is possible for most others. These Master Numbers give a person a great deal of creative energy, and as a result, such people are usually very high-strung. They have a distinct need to channel their creativity into those areas of life that can reflect their potential as well as express the power and influence they are capable of wielding. Finding such outlets and clear life directions is often a challenge, for theirs is a frequency of life energy that most of us do not possess.

Not everyone who has a prominent 11 or 22 in her life lives up to its full promise. Nor can all 11s and 22s sustain the intensity of this numerical vibration all the time. As we shall see, sometimes an 11 will express herself more like a 2 (1+1) and a 22 more like a 4 (2+2).

The Master Number Eleven

Eleven is the number of *illumination*. It is especially connected with the sixth sense, intuition. Real intuition allows us to see the beginning and the end of a situation at the same time. It allows us to perceive the quality of creative energy within its form of outer expression. This gives a person the gift of being able to look at a piece of fruit from the outside and know if it is sweet and ripe on the inside. This is the ability to look at a painting and know what the painter was experiencing in her life while she was painting it. This is the knowledge that allows a person to advise a couple on their marriage because he can see into the nature of that relationship better than the people who are in it.

Number Eleven endows a person with tremendous inspiration and the potential of bringing that inspiration into other people's lives. Number Eleven relates, but this is not the ordinary relating of the Number Two. Yes, of course, Eleven communicates, but the primary type of communication is between the lower and higher selves. It is in this way that Eleven's gifts of intuition and psychic sensibility are received.

A person strongly influenced by the Number Eleven will often take her expanded vision out into the world, usually finding some form of public service or community work to do. It is through the Number Eleven that the individual can see the whole nature of a group or community effort. His own opinion is definitely incorporated into his collective awareness, and he makes sure not to let the demands of his own personal ego stand in the way of the group process. The goal of Number Eleven is to create positive effects on society as a whole.

When a person cannot handle the intensity of this Master Number, she will most likely express the Eleven potential as a Two. This means that instead of working in terms of group relationships, her life may focus on relating more interpersonally. Instead of working spiritually and impersonally with others, she will tend to work more personally on an ordinary level. Nevertheless, the high energy, tension, and potential of this Master Number will still be present in her life.

Keywords: mass communication, group effort, intuition, cooperation, impersonality

The Master Number Twenty-Two

Contained within the 22 is the 4, only raised to a much higher level of expression. Number Twenty-Two is traditionally called the "Master Builder." Like the Four, Twenty-Two is aware of social structure and political law. But unlike his single-digit brother, Twenty-Two bases his building skills on his connection to Universal Structure and Cosmic

Law. In this respect, the Number Twenty-Two confers a distinct interest in metaphysics and the spiritual path to all those influenced by its vibration.

Not all people who have Twenty-Two as one of their major numbers (Destiny, Name, Personality, or Soul Urge) are spiritually evolved saints or altruistic servers of humanity. Yet all Twenty-Twos do things in a big way. This number creates large-scale organizations, world-wide distribution networks, and huge political/economic projects that ideally work to lift people out of material constraints and social limitations.

The Twenty-Two combines the communicative and idealistic approach of the Eleven, then doubles it, adding the power, potential, and understanding of the material plane of Four but raised to a much higher octave. Peter the Great had a Twenty-Two Destiny Number. He was the Russian Czar who, in the late seventeenth century, opened his vast country to Western European culture. Up to this time in history, Russia was mostly cut off from the West due to the lack of roads and the formidable distances between Moscow and major European cities. Peter decided to build St. Petersburg as his new capital, erecting it on the Baltic Sea so that Europeans and Russian merchants could trade. He thus opened his land and people to other ideas and cultures, along with expanding the collective material potential of his vast nation. Peter was not a saint; in fact, like most rulers of his time (or any time), he was also a despot. But the extent and nature of his actions definitely demonstrate the incredible energy of the Number Twenty-Two.

Keywords: expansive power, universal vision, manifestation, structural awareness, *big!*

Your Destiny Number

The Destiny Number (sometimes also called the "Life Path" or "Birth Path") is one of the most important gifts numerology can give you. The meanings contained within your Name Number may change either through marriage or making the decision to change your name. But the Destiny Number remains constant, and as such, it is a consistent influence upon you. Your Destiny Number reveals a great deal about why you are here on Earth. It tells much about what you came to accomplish and the natural direction for your life to take. It is the main pathway or channel for you, providing your major life lessons.

HOW TO FIND YOUR DESTINY NUMBER

Finding your Destiny Number is simple and fun. All it requires is that you know your date of birth and then add all of these numbers and reduce them to a single digit. The only exception to this is if you are born in November (the 11th month), born on the 11th or 22nd of any month, or if the total of your year of birth equals 11 (such as 1910 = 1+9+1+0 = 11) or 22 (such as 1975 = 1+9+7+5 = 22). We always leave these two Master Numbers intact and never reduce them.

Here, then, are the four easy steps you can use to find your own or any other Destiny Number you wish:

1. Change your birth month into a number and reduce it to a single digit (or to the number 11).

January	= 1	July	= 7
February	= 2	August	= 8
March	= 3	September	= 9
April	= 4	October	= 1 (10 = 1+0 = 1)
May	= 5	November	= 11 (Master Number)
June	= 6	December	= 3 (12 = 1+2 = 3)

2. Change your day of birth into a single digit, or leave it if it is a Master Number.

For example, if you were born between the 1st and the 9th of any month, leave your birth day as it is. The same if you were born on the 11th or the 22nd of the month; do not reduce these two numbers. But if you were born on any of the other days, change the number as follows:

10th = 1	20th = 2	30th = 3
12th = 3	21st = 3	31st = 4
13th = 4	23rd = 5	
14th = 5	24th = 6	
15th = 6	25th = 7	
16th = 7	26th = 8	
17th = 8	27th = 9	
18th = 9	28th = 1	
19th = 1	29th = 11 (Please note: 2+9 = 11;	
	do not reduce)	

3. Change your year of birth into a single digit as well, and just as you would do in calculating the month and day, do not reduce the year if it becomes an 11 or a 22. Examples:

$$1922 = 1+9+2+2 = 14 = 5 \ (1+4)$$
$$1934 = 1+9+3+4 = 17 = 8 \ (1+7)$$
$$1946 = 1+9+4+6 = 20 = 2 \ (2+0)$$
$$1954 = 1+9+5+4 = 19 = 1 \ (1+9)$$
$$1966 = 1+9+6+6 = 22 \ (\text{do not reduce})$$

4. Now add up these three numbers of your month, day, and year of birth and (except for 11 and 22) reduce to a single digit (or to 11 or 22). The result is your Destiny Number. After determining this very important factor, please read the corresponding passages on the following pages. Here are some examples:

February 19, 1942:
2nd month + 19th day $(1+9 = 10 = 1) + 1+9+4+2$
$(= 16 = 7)$; $2+1+7 = 10 = 1$. The Destiny Number for this person would be 1.

November 11, 1975:
11th month + 11th day + $1+9+7+5 \ (= 22)$;
$11+11+22 = 44 = 8$. The Destiny Number for this person would be 8.

May 9, 1970:
5th month + 9th day + $1+9+7+0 \ (= 17 = 8)$;
$5+9+8 = 22$. The Destiny Number for this person would be 22.

NUMBER ONE DESTINY NUMBER

The Number One path through life is focused on the development and expression of personal identity. People with this Destiny Number are involved in areas of life that are usually highly competitive, pioneering, or open to further development of ideas, principles, or projects. Such arenas as powerful corporations (especially those seeking to introduce new products and services) and professional sports certainly qualify as natural expressions of a Number One Destiny. The military is another natural form of expression for a person with a Number One Destiny. On another level, metaphysics could also be considered an area of interest, as it certainly deals with unknown territories (of consciousness) and takes a considerable amount of conviction to practice, and the courage to transmute and change! Whatever the area or profession chosen, the Number One will be up against some type of opposition or pressure in the environment, forcing him to use the maximum amount of personal power and will. It is this very use of personal energy that underlies the individualizing effects of a Number One Destiny path.

The strength of one's individuality and character is being forged through forceful self-assertion. The areas of life chosen require one to become a more dynamic personality or else get swallowed up and overwhelmed by those experiences. The latter is not a Number One option! A strong Number One Destiny will refuse to be defeated by any of the outer circumstances of life. Such individuals are achievement-oriented people, constantly driven forward to succeed in their objectives and goals. If they are involved in sports, they are in it to win. If the corporate life is their area of participation, they will aim for status and personal gain. One of their main motivations for success is *recognition*. As a person on the Number One path accomplishes one level of success, he or she will immediately set out to conquer the next, ever seeking a greater sense of personal independence and self-reliance.

The negative side of the Number One Destiny has to do with an avoidance of facing the reality and consequences of the pressures that such a level of motivation and drive brings into one's life. These people may try various forms of escapism, or their natural drive may invert, creating a strong lack of self-esteem. The other extreme has to do with excessive egocentricity and the urge to dominate their environment regardless of others. Their need for recognition and their drive for success will then become over-emphasized to the detriment of their personal and social relationships.

A healthy person on the Number One Destiny path will be able to achieve in life, using his own personal abilities while creating additional opportunities for success. He will be able to do this without manipulating or destroying others, fulfilling his Destiny by becoming an example of positive self-expression and self-empowerment.

Famous Number One Destinies: Martin Luther King, Jr., Walt Disney, Napoleon Bonaparte

NUMBER TWO DESTINY NUMBER

The Number Two path through life is focused on the development and expression of relating and relationships. These individuals are very involved in creating connections with others as well as between people and the environment. They are especially gifted in social situations, as they are usually receptive to other people's needs. On a wider, more political level, the Number Two Destiny can be very ecologically oriented, extending her sensitivity to planetary as well as personal needs. Such an individual has the potential to recognize the state and condition of the world around her, understanding as she does the relativity and interrelationship of life circumstances.

The Number Two Destiny has to do with the recognition of cause and effect. This particular ability can give a person a deep understanding of the resolution of conflicts. It can also endow a person with a clear perception of how such conflicts come about and how to avoid them in the future. In this respect, Number Two Destinies tend to be involved in such professions as diplomat, counselor, mediator, psychologist, and ecologist (for example, park ranger). Whatever the job, the person is a catalyst for bringing two seemingly separate conditions, people, or groups together to work in greater harmony.

The Number Two Destiny person is increasing her sense of receptivity through connection and identification. Working in those areas of life that bring us into more intimate relationship with others encourages an individual to be more tolerant of another's point of view, combine it with her own, and come up with solutions that help all parties involved. The Number Two path is definitely one of human interchange and could be called "the art of creative harmony." The work of the Number Two Destiny is to bring opposites together. She labors to refine her skills of cooperation and relating. Her main motivation for success is increased *connectedness*. The question she asks herself is: "How may I help everyone and everything work together more effectively so that greater growth is achieved?"

The negative side of the Number Two Destiny is just the opposite. It may reveal a person so lacking in the conscious use of the Number Two qualities that she is only slightly aware of others and the conditions in the environment. This lack in character then becomes the main reason for the person's suffering—suffering that often results in unsatisfactory personal relationships. Such a person would tend to be entirely caught up in her own views and unable to integrate any other viewpoints into her life. Alienating others would be easy and solution-making an impossibility. Another negative facet of the Number Two Destiny is coming in contact with the needs of others but being too receptive, too responsive to them. Such individuals can easily become trapped in other people's emotional dramas and take on these feelings as their own. The balance that can then be learned with the Number Two Destiny is how to maintain an integrated sense of oneself while at the same time being supportive and nurturing to others and to the environment.

Famous Number Two Destinies: Gloria Vanderbilt, Jacqueline Kennedy Onassis, Frank Lloyd Wright

NUMBER THREE DESTINY NUMBER

The Number Three path through life is focused on the development and expression of information. Such individuals are involved in the use of language, mathematics, and symbols in order to circulate ideas and knowledge among people. The basic building blocks of ideas are words and sentences, musical notes and chords, numbers and equations, colors and patterns. The areas of life most attractive to people with a Number Three Destiny include writing, journalism, teaching, lecturing, and all forms of education. A Number Three Destiny person is naturally "at home" anywhere there exists the opportunity for the communication of ideas.

The Number Three Destiny indicates a person involved with the circulation of information. This life path keeps one constantly developing new modes of thinking, new ways of communicating, and new opportunities for the use of active intelligence. This path brings many opportunities for travel, as it demands that an individual acquire the tools for interpreting life and sharing those interpretations with others. Number Three Destiny people are thus usually quite bright, talkative, and alive. Their lives are filled with those experiences which bring to them (and to others through them) ideas about how things are put together, how people move and interconnect, and the meaning of current events for people and the planet. In order to communicate all of this clearly and correctly, a person has to develop a well-trained mind. This is definitely the task of a Number Three Destiny. No matter how advanced his or her mental faculties may be, a lifetime with a Number Three Destiny is involved with the development of intelligence and mental capacities. The main stimulation for success in life is the *creation and circulation of ideas*.

The negative side to a Number Three Destiny is a lazy mind. It may indicate a person who is not sufficiently motivated intellectually. Thus it is the cultivation of this vital part of our nature that is the "gift" of these individuals' lifepath experiences. They may find that they have difficulty in learning or avoid participating in those experiences that challenge their intellects. The other extreme of a negative Number Three path is mental arrogance, an over-emphasis on the importance of knowledge (which usually means an under-emphasis on the accumulation of wisdom!). These individuals are so involved with gathering knowledge, often for the sake of power, that they lose sight of all meaning.

Their overly analytical approach to life may cause them to miss the realization that the mind and our intelligence serve to interpret life. They are not life itself.

Famous Number Three Destinies: Barbara Walters, Alice Bailey, Anne Frank

NUMBER FOUR DESTINY NUMBER

The Number Four path through life is focused on the development, expression, and understanding of our social structure. Such individuals are involved with the daily functions of life, working to bring stability and order. The purpose of most social structures is to create a unifying, collective situation so that people's basic needs may be supplied more effectively. In this way, greater individual creativity may surface. At other times, however, certain social and political structures seek to control, direct, and manipulate others so that little individual self-expression is possible.

In all circumstances, a successful society on any level requires a solid foundation and a carefully designed structure. People born with a Number Four Destiny Number are very concerned with these factors. They would most naturally be attracted by those professions that deal with business, politics, the judicial system, as well as such socially oriented programs as public transportation, the educational systems (mostly from an administrative perspective), the police department, and various types of social care. The Number Four Destiny feels most "at home" anywhere the practical concerns of life need to be expressed.

The Number Four Destiny path works to incorporate a sustaining structure and to bring order into our daily life. Such individuals seek to bring this type of stability into the lives of the people around them. They are definitely not dreamy and idealistic in nature and attitude. Their life experiences serve to develop practical applications and pragmatic understandings. They labor to keep their lives in order and to create opportunities for others to be part of an efficient system. Their motivation for success is *practical involvement*. They either work to sustain what has already been developed or they seek to integrate new, more effective ways of running society. The person on the Number Four path would never tear down or change a part of his or her structure without at least putting something new in its place.

The negative side of a Number Four Destiny could be a lack of connection to the processes and patterns of daily life. These people would in effect, lack all the practical sensibilities of the more positive Number Four. Their life lesson would therefore involve learning respect for order, process, structure, and form. They may encounter certain difficulties with the law and/or the status quo of accepted behavior in their society. Such people may find it difficult to sustain a job, especially if that work requires a great deal of routine effort. They would find it generally difficult handling money and participating in the workaday world. The other extreme of the more negative side of the Number Four Destiny describes an individual who is overly cautious, overly conservative, and definitely overly repressed! This is a person who never takes a risk, and whose life has to be totally in control and predictable. Boundaries and structure are wonderful in their positive function. They bring order out of chaos and give direction to both personal and planetary evolution and growth. Negatively, they stifle the power and potential of our individual possibilities.

Famous Number Four Destinies: Julius Caesar, Leonardo da Vinci, Francis Bacon

NUMBER FIVE DESTINY NUMBER

The Number Five path through life is focused on the development and expression of new experiences. Such individuals are involved in circumstances outside the accepted patterns of life in the practical, daily world. Anything that creates a sense of reaching out, expansion, or newness falls under this Destiny Number's influence. This includes the travel industry (agents, airplane attendants, pilots, and drivers), inventors, social reformers, explorers, scientists, and mystics. Whatever the occupation, its inherent quality calls for reaching past previous boundaries into new and potentially boundless areas of life.

People on the Number Five path are searching for anything that makes life more stimulating, dynamic, and expansive, both for themselves and for others. They have already absorbed the essence of the Number Four Destiny and have within them the inner experiences of the social structures of society. Their urge is to find those situations that can be used to improve the existing conditions within their own lives and in society generally. The primary motivation for their actions is *freedom*, and their process involves *change*.

The Number Five Destiny path describes people who want to make a difference in their own and others' quality of experience. We could say that the invention of the light bulb as an extension of candlelight is a Number Five Destiny. The mystic when he seeks to move into new areas of consciousness and the artist when she seeks to expand her creative potential are both under the influence of the Five

Destiny Number. Number Five is the path of the visionary who sets forth to materialize his or her vision.

The negative side of the Number Five Destiny has to do with a lack of interest in such expansive opportunities. These individuals find that although they may come in contact with new life circumstances, they approach such situations with fear and denial. These people would tend to struggle against their own growth, living out their lives in ways that suppress growth. The other extreme of this negative side to the Number Five Destiny gives too great an expansive urge. This can result in chaos as well as an obsessive and fanatical attitude about one's visions. Such people may thus become overly idealistic about their possibilities and disappointed when their dreams do not come true. When they have just enough practicality as a quality of their character, they can then share their creative insights and expanded potential for the benefit of many others.

Famous Number Five Destinies: Charles Darwin, Madame Blavatsky, James Joyce

THE NUMBER SIX DESTINY NUMBER

The Number Six path through life is focused on the development and expression of artistic creativity, harmony, and love. Such individuals are involved in those areas of life that deal with creatively expressing what is inside themselves. Art is an important reflection of how we experience life. Often it is hard to explain how we feel solely through logic and verbal communication. The Number Six path includes life circumstances that stimulate one's urge to express some of the more abstract facets and feelings of life. The Number Six path would thus include such professions as painting, sculpture, music, the theater, graphics, and interior design. In essence, the Number Six Destiny involves *beauty*. Whatever the career, people with a Number Six Destiny are attempting to swim deeply into the human psyche and bring into the world some of the colorful experiences (both beautiful and dreadful) that define how we live. In this respect, we can find a number of psychologists, as well as astrologers, numerologists, and tarot readers, on the Six path.

Individuals with this Destiny Number are developing refinement of their creative skills. They are often especially gifted with the ability to work with patterns and shapes of all sorts, be they sound, rhythm, color, archetypes, or paradigms. Their eyes see all the variations in which life may express itself.

There is an ancient metaphysical saying: "God creates geometrically." This idea fuels the Number Six path, as the main motivations for success in life for the Number Six Destiny are *balance* and *beauty*. This is seen in the life of an artist, trying to produce the ultimate "masterpiece" by creating an expression in color and form that reflects perfectly a feeling or emotion. Number Six is at work in the life of the psychologist or the counseling astrologer who portrays in the shape of symbols and words how his client's subconscious functions. The more understanding and clarity that a person on the Number Six path can unfold, the closer that person comes to creating his particular "masterpiece."

The negative side of the Number Six Destiny results in the lack of a strong creative impulse. Sometimes the person doesn't use his or her latent potential at all. Such individuals may express the harmonious attributes contained within the Six but do not necessarily add anything of beauty of their own to the world around them. Their life lesson involves learning how to express themselves through becoming attuned to their inner resources and then finding those experiences in life that stimulate their creative self-expression.

Famous Number Six Destinies: Albert Einstein, Friedrich Nietzsche, Eleanor Roosevelt

NUMBER SEVEN DESTINY NUMBER

The Number Seven path through life is focused on the development and expression of philosophical and scientific concepts. Such individuals are involved in the systematic understanding of ideas. Their life experiences allow them to transform the vague and abstract into practical applications. It is then that their ideas and concepts turn into those new sociological patterns and products that affect our daily life. Their most likely professions are scientist, theorist, philosopher, metaphysician, researcher, engineer, technician, school administrator, politician, and clergy. No matter what their actual line of endeavor, the type of work most oriented to a Number Seven Destiny path almost always involves the refinement and integration of new ideas.

In this respect, the Number Seven Destiny path brings into one's life opportunities to use reason as a tool for the conversion of abstract visions into a more practical form. Let us take the example of an engineer who has a Seven Destiny Number. The engineer lives in a middle-sized town that is ripe for growth. He understands that the town would thrive more if it could increase the amount of commerce passing through it. There are two problems that have to be overcome before the engineer can implement his vision of progress for his town. The first is if there is a group of conservative townspeople who oppose any growth. The second is if there is a river going through the town that cuts off traffic routes, but, if opened, would make additional trade possible.

The engineer resolves the first problem by holding town meetings where he shares his visions with others, gaining support for his concepts. This accomplished, he now has the collective backing to deal with the second question, the river. Here the engineer uses his skills to design a bridge which is then built by a combination of local, state, and federal funds. I am, of course, simplifying matters, but I believe that this example explains the life circumstances encountered by our Number Seven Destiny friend. As we can see, the main motivation for success for a Seven life path is *development*. Such people are continually using their strong analytical power to document the patterns they see, and to develop their insights from the data they gather. They may then work to create those methodical, practical changes which make the systems in their environment run better.

The negative side of the Number Seven Destiny is a lack of rationality. Such people have a difficult time using logic or harnessing their problem-solving abilities. Their life experiences bring them in contact with difficult situations, forcing them to develop practical discernment and a more logical approach to their environment. The more exaggerated aspect of a Number Seven Destiny is the tendency to be overly analytical. In this case, the approach to life may be so critical and super-rational that they encounter more problems than might otherwise be necessary. This is what happens when the separative tendencies of the lower mind are not integrated into the inclusive element of the heart.

Famous Number Seven Destinies: Joseph Pulitzer, Fyodor Dostoevsky, Josephine Baker

NUMBER EIGHT DESTINY NUMBER

The Number Eight path through life is focused on the creation and expression of material comfort. Such individuals are involved in those areas of life that produce the material goods we need or want. People with a Number Eight Destiny are especially involved in the realm of business—the bigger the enterprise, the larger and more influential the corporation, the better! These are the bankers, financiers, stockbrokers (the Stock Market is an excellent example of a Number Eight area of life), investors, senior executives, and presidents of companies.

The Number Eight path concentrates on creating material products and possibilities. It brings those experience to life that allow a person to develop and market an object or service to the public. The Number Eight Destiny person may either invent this product or further refine the work of scientists and researchers (Number Seven Destiny). People on the Number Eight life path may be very astute in the ways they are able to obtain financial backing. They are also good at organizing others to help them run their businesses, and create the abundance that comes into their lives. The Number Eight path gives one the chance to evolve an understanding of how to use every possible avenue of opportunity to market one's creative output. Eights are aware of the power of advertising and are keen entrepreneurs. The main motivation for success in life is *productivity*, and, consequently, we find many high-powered men and women born with this destiny path in life.

The automobile industry, telephone companies, shipping consortiums, and the Stock Market are perfect examples of the types and level of business that appeal to the Number Eight Destiny. These people are not petty in their orientation, preferring large-scale enterprises. Whenever possible, a Number Eight path will stimulate the opportunity to manufacture products that can shape whole societies. Coca-Cola and McDonald's would be good examples of this type of mega-enterprise with strong sociological overtones. Naturally, not every person on this destiny path has the capabilities or the interest to become a superstar CEO. But the Number Eight certainly offers the possibility!

The negative side to the Number Eight Destiny is, of course, just the reverse of this promise: a lack of creative ability in the material world. This person is not capable of establishing or running a business venture. His destiny is involved in working with money and the material plane so that he may eventually learn how to transform his ideas into profitable forms. The exaggerated aspect of a Number Eight Destiny is easy to surmise: it describes a person who is overly materialistic. The Number Eight Destiny has the potential to reap the rewards of large amounts of money and the physical security that comes with material abundance. But a person may become so enamored of money (and the power that comes with it) that she becomes insensitive to basic human needs and values. And, of course, how much money is enough? Even though she may have millions, she can easily get trapped in the mind-set of never having enough. Imelda Marcos always thought she was bare-footed—even with more than 3000 pairs of shoes!

Famous Number Eight Destinies: Richard Nixon, Joan Crawford, Pablo Picasso, Lucille Ball

NUMBER NINE DESTINY NUMBER

The Number Nine path through life is focused on the development and expression of idealism. Such individuals are involved in those philosophical and teaching arenas by which the communication of ideas stimulates people's awareness of the meaning of life. This activity is often connected to the alleviation of sociological problems. Here we find philanthropists, social reformers, clergy, ministers, and socially responsible and ecologically aware groups and organizations. Archaeologists and anthropologists also fall into this category when these men and women are dedicated to preserving and/or uncovering the universal values contained within different cultures. Whatever the occupation, its main purpose is the creation of greater understanding among people for the alleviation of human suffering.

The primary motivation in life is *service*, resulting in the resolution of social ills and human oppression. Such organizations and individuals as the Red Cross, Mahatma Gandhi, the Peace Corps, the Women's Movement, and the Civil Rights Movement are all examples that fit under the description of a Number Nine Destiny. All "Green Party" work—Save the Whales, Save the Rain Forests, Save the Children—also falls under the Nine Destiny Number's vibration. This path brings to an individual a series of life experiences that may have an effect on his social awareness. Thus he may be in a position to aid society and benefit the planet—not a bad job to have!

There are many tensions in the world that require increased awareness on everyone's part. In this respect, people with a Number Nine Destiny are inclined to write pamphlets and books, do documentary television shows, organize demonstrations and reform groups, and give lectures and speeches that bring important social issues to the forefront of our consciousness. This work may also be done as an author, artist, politician, or movie producer. The important thing here is one's attitude, as the Number Nine Destiny serves to bring about *social awareness.*

The negative side of a Number Nine Destiny is insensitivity to social and world issues. The person is either ignorant of or denies the existence of world problems and the need to resolve ecological challenges. The exaggerated aspect of this destiny is a person who is a "bleeding heart." Everything is seen as a problem, and such a person becomes overly sensitive to all issues. He may take on certain social problems but would tend to do so more idealistically than realistically. In essence, he becomes an "armchair philosopher."

Famous Number Nine Destinies: Mahatma Gandhi, Confucius, Shirley MacLaine

NUMBER ELEVEN DESTINY NUMBER

The Number Eleven path through life is focused on the development and expression of expansive participation in the community. Such individuals are involved in areas of life that affect society in subtle but pervasive ways. They choose careers that include schoolteacher and other forms of educational occupation, social worker, mayor, town counselor, spiritual worker, astrologer, and psychic. Anything that deals with community, such as clubs (Girl Scouts, Boy Scouts), programs (PAL boxing, YMCA, YWCA), and political work, with the aim of effecting the well-being of an entire community, fits under the Number Eleven path. School programs such as teaching, developing the education curriculum, sports events, and clubs are included under the Number Eleven path.

People doing this kind of work are concerned about the people and places where they live. Their primary motivation for achievement is *collective well-being*. They serve to make their towns and cities more beautiful and humane through the creation of parks and recreational areas, as well as through cleaning and up-grading downtrodden areas of their communities. They may coach a local Little League team, or join or lead their local Kiwanis or Lions Club. Setting up and sustaining a local "Neighborhood Watch" program is also the kind of activity that would be most natural to an Eleven Destiny. In the case of spiritual workers on the Eleven life path, they are functioning to expand people's consciousness (very subtle and challenging work indeed!). This expansion can only lead to greater caring and mutual support. The Number Eleven is a "Master Number." Those people living under its influence are generally more aware of this need for communal love and cooperation than most others. As a result, they may often work to pass on the benefits of their understanding through some type of counseling practice.

The negative side of the Number Eleven Destiny is a lack of care and concern about community and general social conditions. This person would tend not to be involved in community projects, to go to parades and festivals, or to contribute to the community in any way. This results in the antithesis of the positive Eleven vibration and causes social alienation and loneliness. The lesson for such an individual is the integration of the personal within the scope of the collective. This activity forces an awakening of the heart. The more exaggerated aspect of an Eleven

Destiny Number is loss of the sense of balance between one's personal and community lives. The person would find that he becomes so overly involved in the community that his own family or intimate relationships suffer as a result.

Famous Number Eleven Destinies: Groucho Marx, Paul Simon, Prince Charles

NUMBER TWENTY-TWO DESTINY NUMBER

The Number Twenty-Two path through life is focused on development and expression on national or planetary levels. Such individuals are involved in those areas of life that affect the entire nation in which they live. Presidents, premiers, emperors, kings and queens, diplomats, political administrators, U.S. senators and representatives—all work under the influence of the Number Twenty-Two Destiny path.

People working under the Number Twenty-Two Destiny vibration are often in a position to make decisions that affect and influence very large numbers of people. Their primary motivation for success in life has to do with *national* or *collective interests*. They are concerned with such topics as socialized health care, federal funding, and the administration of the military. They seek to represent their country in talks dealing with international trade (in which they may certainly be accompanied by quite a few Number Eight Destiny people!). The Number Twenty-Two Destiny path may include people who decide the nature of war or peace. Yet such people may also be artists or poets whose work influences the cultural life of their nation. These extremely talented and powerful people are the creators of those images and ideas that become the symbols that define a culture.

The negative side of the Number Twenty-Two Destiny has to do with the misuse of power. A person with so much control (and an underdeveloped heart or sense of the Soul) can easily become manipulative and domineering. It is then that dictators and tyrants emerge and tyrannize whole populations. These Twenty-Two Destiny paths give rise to individuals on any social level who care little about the good of others and are motivated solely by their own ambitions.

Famous Number Twenty-Two Destinies: Peter the Great, Grandma Moses, Joseph Kennedy, Marie Curie, Eugene McCarthy, Annie Besant, Mark Twain

KEYWORDS

To aid our understanding of the Destiny Numbers, the following list of keywords and phrases may be helpful. The first column is obviously the Destiny Number itself. The second column shows *where* (in what area of life) an individual is working out that destiny. The third column shows *what* the individual is doing in order to gain a deeper understanding of his or her Destiny or to express that Destiny path more fully.

Examples:
Individuals with a Number One Destiny are working out their life path *in themselves* and gaining a deeper understanding of their destiny path *by asserting themselves.*

Individuals with a Number Two Destiny are working out their life path *in relationships* and gaining a deeper understanding of their destiny *by connecting and relating* with others.

One	in themselves	by asserting themselves
Two	in relationships	by connecting and relating
Three	in ideas	by working with patterns of information
Four	in social structures	by being practical
Five	in new experiences	by searching and exploring
Six	in creativity	by being artistic
Seven	in research and discovery	by being contemplative and analytical
Eight	in business	by producing material products
Nine	in service	by helping others
Eleven	in community	by serving and defining the needs of the group
Twenty-Two	in collective work	by working with the needs of the whole

Your Personal Year Number

Everything in the Universe moves in cycles. The moon circles about the Earth, and we see its cycles expressed in its various phases. The Earth circles about the Sun, and its cycle is expressed by the four seasons. All the planets orbit around the Sun, and it is the relationship of their cycles to the Earth and to one another that forms the basis of the ancient science of astrology. (For further reference, please see the *Pocket Guide to Astrology*, by Alan Oken [The Crossing Press, 1996].)

Numerologists also see the events of human life unfolding in cycles. As we just discovered, the Destiny Number is one of the most important numerological guides, as it tells us so much about the nature of our life and its proper direction. In addition to the Destiny Number, our primary life path indicator, there is a vital nine-year cycle. Every year in this cycle is characterized by certain traits and indications of a particular numerical vibration, from one through nine. This is your Personal Year. This Number will reveal to you a great deal about the influences, characteristics, and events of any given year within this nine-year period and can be a source of much helpful information for every calendar year of your life. Your Personal Year Number is therefore a wonderful thing to know, and all you need to determine it is your month and day of birth plus the number of the current year. Once you obtain your Personal Year Number, you will then have an excellent guide to determining what you can do to benefit most from living in harmony with your natural cycle.

If you just follow four simple steps outlined below, you will have calculated your Personal Year Number. After you have this number at hand, please read the corresponding passages in this chapter. It's also a good idea to go back in time and check out how this nine-year cycle repeats itself in your life. Let's say that 1995 was a "6" Personal Year for you. After studying what is written here about a "6" Personal Year (as well as the Number Six in general), try to think back nine years to 1986 and see if you can find the similarities in your life circumstances. Do the same for 1994 and 1985, 1993 and 1984, as these years will also have the same Personal Number vibration. This is yet another way that numerology can lead you to a deeper understanding of yourself and the life you are co-creating with the Universe.

HOW TO FIND YOUR PERSONAL YEAR NUMBER

To find your Personal Year Number:

1. Determine the number of any calendar year and reduce it to a single digit. For example:

> 1996 = 1+9+9+6 = 25 = 7
> 1997 = 1+9+9+7 = 26 = 8
> 1999 = 1+9+9+9 = 28 = 10 = 1
> 2000 = 2+0+0+0 = 2 = 2

2. Take your day of birth and reduce it to a single digit (19th =10=1, 24th = 6).

3. Do the same for your birth month.

4. Add these three numbers and reduce all of them to a single digit. For example, if you wanted to calculate your

Personal Year Number for 1996 and your birthday falls on March 2nd, you would do as follows:

March 2, 1996
3+2+7 = 12 = 3 (Personal Year Number)

5. The Personal Year cycle consists of nine years. In this case the Master Numbers 11 and 22 are also reduced to the single digits 2 and 4, respectively.

Please note: Your Personal Year begins at your birthday on the year in question and ends the day before your birthday of the following year. Thus for our example above, the "3" Personal Year is in effect from March 2, 1996, to March 1, 1997. It does not matter even if you were born in November or December. Calculate your Personal Year as indicated above and know that whatever Number Year may result is in effect from birthday to birthday. A careful reading of the descriptive passages about each of these Personal Year Numbers will give you some very helpful clues on how to make each and every Personal Year a most successful one for you.

NUMBER ONE PERSONAL YEAR

This is a year in which you will devote a lot of your time and effort to defining and expressing who you are and what you seek to do in life. It is a year for the development of your sense of self and the assertion of your individuality. You will thus be involved with those experiences that can:

1. Increase your awareness of your strengths and weaknesses;
2. Help you to recognize your habit patterns;
3. Define your personal likes and dislikes;
4. Refine your talents and gifts;
5. Develop inner power and resources.

During a One Personal Year, you may also find that you have to deal with issues that reflect how and when you are *not* being yourself. Where are you compromising your inner and outer growth? Are there new interests and hobbies that need to be cultivated in order to further your own creativity? The Number One Year should usher in those circumstances and conditions that create the impulse for a person not only to stand on his or her own feet, but to use them in a quick "Forward March!"

NUMBER TWO PERSONAL YEAR

This is a year for developing personal relationships and creating cooperative efforts. It is during a Number Two Personal Year that we can increase the quality of our connections to others in all facets of our relationships: at work, at home, and in the world at large. You will find that your life is bringing to you those experiences which allow you to refine how you are connecting with others. You will be given the opportunity to understand with greater precision the nature of the subtle emotional and psychological patterns that condition your ties with others.

The "Law of Circulation" is at work during this time in terms of sharing and the important art of give and take in your relationships. In this respect, you will find that one of the greatest lessons a Number Two Year can offer is the opportunity for balance in your interpersonal relationships. This is a year for the development of emotional sensitivity. Your experiences during the previous One Personal Year should have given you enough sense of yourself that you may give a great deal of yourself to others without losing your integrity.

NUMBER THREE PERSONAL YEAR

This is a year for the development of your mental abilities. It is a time in which you will want to study, accumulate new ideas, increase communication skills, and advance your capabilities with mechanical instruments and/or tools (computers, musical instruments, etc.). You are creating additional models and concepts to interpret and communicate your understanding of life. These new skills give you the opportunity for career advancement.

It is during a Three Personal Year that you may find yourself exposed to many different types of information that you will have to process and integrate. You will find that writing, speaking, teaching, and, if you are so inclined, composing music are vehicles to help your creative self-expression at this time. This is certainly a year in which you can reach out to others through such skills and relate what you are feeling and thinking, thus refining your ability to communicate. You will therefore find that you will be spending more time than usual out and about in social situations. The more that you are able to express yourself, the more you are also able to increase your awareness of other people's ideas and viewpoints. Thus the Number Three Personal Year is an excellent opportunity for social maturation and integration.

NUMBER FOUR PERSONAL YEAR

This is a year for you to develop your practical life skills. During this time, you may well find yourself hard at work at a job that gives you the experiences necessary for the cultivation of pragmatism. Your daily life concerns (food, shelter, clothing) will be of great importance. This does not necessarily indicate a year of lack. In fact, you may find that it can be during a Number Four Personal Year that you come into contact with the ability to structure your life in such a way that your material abundance increases.

You are in a period in which your involvement with life is centered on the ability to create a more definitive sense of your personal responsibilities. It is a time that teaches the awareness of personal boundaries and perimeters so that you can perfect the ways you use your time and personal resources. In this respect, you may be learning how to make money in particular, while budgeting and administering the use of your life energy in general. You are recognizing what you can and cannot accomplish at your present level of education, personal skills, and practical understanding of life. In addition, you are learning about order and organization. This may take form and focus in some deliberate effort at self-discipline, resulting in a vision of those new experiences you will want to cultivate during your Five Personal Year.

NUMBER FIVE PERSONAL YEAR

This is a year of personal expansiveness. It is a period in your life in which you will reach into the unknown, experimenting and trying something different. There is a strong urge to have those experiences that create a different vision of how life can be lived. A Number Five Personal Year ushers in a time in which a person is breaking free from her usual routines and searching for new adventure and opportunity.

You may thus find yourself driven by a surging curiosity and a definite discontent with the way things are. If you have an interest in something, this is the year in which you will investigate it. If you are finding that your life is limited at work or in your relationship, it will be during the Number Five Year that you may find yourself wandering about in search of greater self-satisfaction in these areas. This is a time for expressing your independence and personal freedom. You will certainly not want to be caged in or held down. If there are restrictive patterns in your personality that need to be worked through, if there are limitations to your creativity in your environment, this is the time you will work to break out and break free. Your individual growth and development takes place during this Five Personal Year in your attempts through such challenges to dissolve the status quo in your life.

NUMBER SIX PERSONAL YEAR

This is a year in which you will develop your creative skills and have the opportunity to find a greater sense of peace and harmony within yourself. The new lessons gained from your Five Personal Year can be integrated into your life. You will find that you want to bring these added experiences into your environment and enrich those around you. Family and friends take on additional importance as you seek to expand yourself harmoniously and lovingly with those closest to you.

You have found a greater sense of peace and inner confidence. The tensions involved in personal growth have reached a certain plateau, as you have more vehicles to release the creative impulses within yourself. There is an intimate connection between the creative process and becoming more in touch with personal stability. More often than not, an artist or writer is using his skills as vehicles for the release of inner ideas and feelings. The Six Personal Year is a time for such a release, and with it comes the urge to use your added talents and abilities to help create a more beautiful world. This is your year for healing and wholeness, harmony and right human relationships. It is a time in which you pause in the intensity of the urge for greater self-fulfillment and express what you have already achieved. This gives you the opportunity to mend relationships and help others in your family and social circumstances as well. People around you will sense this inner balance and peace, and you will find encouragement coming from many different quarters in your life.

NUMBER SEVEN PERSONAL YEAR

This is a year for renewed efforts at personal development. During this period, you will find the urge to delve deeper into your inner core and discover the nature of your philosophical or spiritual beliefs as well as the true meaning of your life values. The Seven Personal Year allows you to systematically review your understanding of yourself and life in general. It is a contemplative and reflective year, one in which you can open yourself to a more profound sense of self-realization.

This can be a year for a "vision quest." You will find that such inner searching leads to the creation of deep changes in the context of your life, yielding insights that result in new ways of approaching your deepest yearnings. Philosophical and scientific inquiry into life's hidden truths will become very important to you during this year. Those with a mystical bent may find themselves involved with metaphysics and religion. Those with a more analytical mind will find this search more in the area of the natural sciences.

In either case, a person is developing higher qualities of their mental abilities in order to isolate and solve particular problems. This gives rise to the evolution of personal methodologies and an increase in one's ability to organize ideas. The Number Seven Personal Year can be a very constructive time in your life. You will find that you are in a position to tap into your greater potentials. You are building new mental and psychic structures in order to handle life with greater insight and efficiency.

NUMBER EIGHT PERSONAL YEAR

This is a year for personal prosperity. It is a time for the development of your practical life values and the construction of your business interests and ventures. You would be well advised at this period to use some of your creative energy to invent a "product," find financial backers for your ideas, organize the running of a commercial enterprise, and bring into physical form whatever it is you are trying to create.

You can expand the economic side of your life through using your various social and business connections to present this product to society. Advertise and let people know what it is that you have to offer. A Number Eight Personal Year is a time when you can reap the rewards from previous work and efforts. This is also a good year for examining the nature of your investments. You can create some additional returns now through placing an intelligent focus on your goals for practical achievements. You have the opportunity to increase the amount of material security you possess and create a higher standard of living for yourself and those close to you. If, however, you have not put the needed work and time into your business or have not developed the understanding from which to profit from your creative ventures, an Eight Personal Year could be a financial challenge.

NUMBER NINE PERSONAL YEAR

This is a year of completion for you. The Nine Personal Year is the last in this important time cycle. It is during this year that you will experience a certain finality to all the work you have done in your life to bring what you have learned, created, built, and produced to a point of conclusion and integration. Your next birthday will usher in a Number One Personal Year and the process will begin all over again, ideally on a higher turn of the evolutionary spiral.

Your life lessons should have brought an increase in your level of understanding and degree of emotional sensitivity, and in the profundity of the wisdom you have been able to glean from your experiences. You can now examine the gains and losses from your work efforts and see how you can make future improvements. The Nine Personal Year is a time for personal "regrouping" so that you may express yourself with greater integrity, strength, and vision. If you have acquired enough creative tools and invested something of yourself in the world. then the Number Nine Personal Year is one of involvement. You can then use your developed skills and insight in order to have a positive effect on the world around you.

If this is not the case, and you find that you have insufficiently prepared yourself for a larger task in life, you will then find that the Number Nine Personal Year can be used for deep reflection and introspection. You would do well to step back and ascertain what needs to be experienced and developed. You may then continue on refreshed and renewed under the impulse of the coming One Personal Year.

And it goes on....

Your Success Year Number

You will have a major year in your life every time your Personal Year Number is the same as your Destiny Number. This means that the characteristics and events of that year will be especially powerful for you. By mastering your understanding of the basic meanings of the numbers and adding this to your knowledge of both your Destiny and Personal Year Numbers, you will be able to derive the greatest benefit and the most rewards from these Success Years. Determining these years is made even easier as there is no new formula to learn. All you need are your Destiny and Personal Year Numbers, and these you already have. That's all it takes, plus a reading of the appropriate passages in this chapter. Obviously, such peak years in your life are not going to yield their greatest potential on "automatic pilot." You are the pilot and your life is the plane. A study of numerology (as well as astrology and the tarot) can certainly give us a map to where we are going, but it is always up to us as individuals to learn how high to fly.

As mentioned above, a Success Year occurs for you when your Personal Year Number is the same as your Destiny Number. For example, we have learned that if a person was born on April 17, 1969, he or she would have a "1" Destiny Number (April = 4, 17 = 8, 1969 = 25 = 7). Then adding the three numbers we get: 4+8+7 = 19 = 1+9 = 10 = 1.

If we look at 1996, we will see that this is also a "1" Personal Year for our imaginary friend. When we take April

17 and add 1996, we also come up with a "1" (4+8+7 = 19 = 10 = 1). Because the Personal Year Number matches the Destiny Number for our lucky friend, 1996 has the potential of being one of his Success Years, with the qualities of success expressed through the vibrations of the Number One. In this case, the individual in question would likely be acknowledged for some type of personal achievement or advancement in life.

Please keep in mind that a Success Year is going to contain the same events and circumstances you would expect to find in the Personal Year of the same number—but much more so! Remember that the force and power of the Destiny Number are also involved. The keyword is "emphasis," and the emphasis will be on the numerical quality of the Success Year Number.

Success Years also move in a cycle of nine. Thus if your Destiny Number is an 11, you should reduce this to a 2 and read the respective passage; likewise, a Twenty-Two Destiny will correspond to a 4 Success Year. Keep in mind that Master Number Destinies always contain a deeper level of intensity and a wider scope of application than numbers One through Nine.

NUMBER ONE SUCCESS YEAR

You have achieved a certain degree of self-awareness that pays off for you during this year. Now is the time in which you can assert your special talents and abilities through your own unique form of self-expression. This is not a year to neglect your capabilities and potentialities but to strive forward and make the most of who you are. Clarity of direction, strength of purpose, and determination are all characteristics of a One Success Year. Use them wisely and use them well, and you can make quite an impression on your environment. This is a time of greatly increased self-confidence and a rooted sense of personal power.

NUMBER TWO SUCCESS YEAR

People often come to a numerologist, astrologer, or tarot reader and ask the same important question: "When can I meet my 'soul mate'? Where is that 'special other'?" Success in personal relationships comes with a Number Two Success Year. You will find that your life holds many opportunities for profound connections with others. If you are already with your life partner or another "significant other," then look for an even deeper connection in your relationship. If you are still searching, a Number Two Year should bring you into contact with possibilities for a major connection to another person. But the energy of a Number Two Success Year is not confined within the scope of purely personal intimacies. Look for major expansion in all forms of relationship and in your ability to reach people with personal truth and honesty.

NUMBER THREE SUCCESS YEAR

Opportunities come into life that deepen your ability to use accumulated knowledge and acquired tools. You will find that what you have already achieved educationally, and in the development of intellectual skills in general, really pays off for you. These skills can lead to career and social advancement. Your ability to communicate and reach other people takes on an added dimension as you move forward in society, teaching and sharing. This act of circulating your information, talents, and general know-how results in any number of social and personal rewards. One of the most important will be the satisfaction you receive in seeing how what you have learned up to this stage in your life can be so beneficial to those around you.

NUMBER FOUR SUCCESS YEAR

Whatever your job or career, this is a year for strong potential gain and advancement. You can perfect your current level of achievement and solidify your position in life. You are ready to assume greater responsibilities and incorporate more material abundance into your existence. In order to fulfill the potential contained in this year, you would have had to master the lessons of form and structure. What comes to you during a Four Success Year are opportunities to prove your abilities in these areas. If you have not developed some degree of personal self-discipline, a Number Four Success Year will bring these lessons home to you in no uncertain terms. You will then find yourself in a position to learn these lessons with speed and efficiency, as much is at stake in their timely accomplishment.

NUMBER FIVE SUCCESS YEAR

Travel and adventure characterize this important time in your life. Less involved with experimentation, rebelliousness, and the need for individual freedom as the Five Personal Year, the Five Success Year allows much more focus in the choices you make in your urge for self-expansion. You are actively seeking those experiences that widen your capabilities and enlarge your talents, but there is the tendency to be less emotionally impulsive and more concretely attached to those areas you wish to open and explore. There is precision in your desire for freedom, and conscious direction in your movements.

NUMBER SIX SUCCESS YEAR

Harmony, beauty, balance, and love all take on a special significance during this Success Year. There should be a great deal of serenity as you move through life expressing yourself with a heightened degree of creativity. You are in touch with your roots and consciously integrating your talents and abilities. This results in greater success in your chosen field of life work and/or artistic self-expression. Benefits from your efforts and actions can come into your domestic life and into your other close relationships as well. You seem to be a source of great comfort to the people around you and may easily find yourself inspired spiritually as well as artistically during this very important year of your life.

NUMBER SEVEN SUCCESS YEAR

Your efforts at increasing your understanding of life are renewed and supported during this Success Year. Although not the most sociable period, you will nevertheless find that spending time alone has its rewards. If there have been some inventive urges within you during the past few years, it will be during a Seven Success Year that you manifest their potential. You may find that your mind is especially analytical as you strive to perfect your connection to a profound philosophy or belief system. Your need to come in contact with the hidden forces of life may easily lead you to a committed study of the metaphysical path, or if the intellect is where you feel your special calling, you will be able to make substantial advances in any chosen field having to do with science, computers, or research.

NUMBER EIGHT SUCCESS YEAR

It is during this year that opportunities for material growth become quite bountiful. You will find that all your previous investments and hard work can pay off handsomely for you. This is a year in which many people reach a pinnacle in their careers and create avenues for even more success in the future. It is easy to network through professional and business contacts in order to uncover the best opportunities in your particular field of endeavor. You do not have to make all these efforts on your own, as the doors open for you, swinging wide to reveal the rewards awaiting your hard work. In order to prepare for an Eight Success Year, you should take advantage of the stability found in the Six Personal Year and the introspection available in the previous Seven Personal Year. These experiences when combined, give you the necessary maturity for the potential advancement in life that is available at this time.

NUMBER NINE SUCCESS YEAR

For many people, this year brings a profound spiritual awakening. It seems that many of the seemingly separate pieces of your life fuse together, bringing you a deep sense of personal integration and wholeness. When extended into life in general, the Number Nine Success Year helps you to see the continuity of the world around you, the essential unity existing among all the races and nations of humanity, and allows you to perceive the endless cycles of nature at work. In this respect, the Nine Success Year culminates any efforts you have been making towards a greater spiritual reality. Once accepted, the gifts of this year form the backdrop to the projection of a now more universalized self into the world awaiting you in your next One Personal Year.

The Numbers in Your Name

Your name holds a great many keys to your individuality. It is first and foremost the sound with which you most closely identify yourself. It is the word around which you have built your personal identity and the word others use to identify you to themselves. When other people hear or think of your name, your image and everything associated with it comes to mind.

At certain stages in your life, your name changes. As a child, you are often given a nickname. This is frequently a description of something about you like the color of your hair ("Red"), a personality trait ("Princess"), your status in the family ("Junior"), or a diminutive of your first name ("Bobby").

As we mature and our inner image develops, we want the world to see those changes reflected in our name. A time comes for many of us when we say, "Please, don't call me Curly anymore. My name is Steven." For the first twenty-five years of my life, I was "Alan C. Oken." I changed my name to the simpler "Alan Oken," as I felt at the time very self-expressive and direct. I wanted my name to be easier to remember and shorter to say. I felt that the "C" gave my name a heavier sound, and I wanted to be freer to express myself. I didn't know at the time that "Alan C. Oken" was a Number Four name (solidification, limitation, responsibility) and "Alan Oken" is a Number One (individuality, independence, assertiveness)!

The most obvious name changes occur when we adjust them to suit our social needs. This comes about for women when they marry. In this respect, a women who has had several marriages will have the numerical vibration in her name changing several times in one lifetime. As we will soon discover, these name changes bring into life more than just different husbands! They bring to us a totally different series of life lessons, challenges, and accomplishments.

Our evolving social patterns give us other opportunities to create new names. Many modern married couples join both their names together into a hyphenated last name. Alice Peterson marries Harold Blake and she becomes Alice Peterson-Blake and her husband becomes Harold Blake-Peterson. This brings a different number and its consequences into both people's lives. Other people take on names that express their spiritual path or a quality of human nature they feel they embody. I have met many a Thomas, Sandra, and Richard who now call themselves Shanti, Peace, or Sunshine.

Media personalities are very likely to change their names, as public image is an essential quality to their stardom. Think of the very talented rock star "Prince." Prince is a very powerful name, as it is a Master Number 11. This number is associated with large-scale communication, allowing a person to reach great masses of people. In his urge for increased public recognition, Prince changed his name to a symbol, and from a numerological point of view, has given himself a "name" which means "0"! It is true that the "0" indicates "The All and Everything," but it is an "all and everything" that has no form, no manifestation. It is pure potential without shape, without direction. I think that Prince should have consulted a numerologist before he made the change, as I believe his public image has decreased considerably since he erased his name.

HOW TO FIND YOUR NAME NUMBER

Once you determine your Name Number, you will have an essential key to the way you express yourself in the many outer experiences of your life. Use the accompanying table to find the numerical equivalents of the letters in your name. This is done as follows:

1	2	3	4	5	6	7	8	9
A	B	C	D	E	F	G	H	I
J	K	L	M	N	O	P	Q	R
S	T	U	V	W	X	Y	Z	

Table of Letter–Number Equivalents

1. Write out your entire name and place the number for each letter below the corresponding letter. Begin with using your original, given name. Do not include any numbers or abbreviations that may occur after your name, such as Jr., Sr., Esq., III, etc. *It is your given, full name at birth that reveals your fundamental, initial life expression.* This is the name you should use at the outset of your work in numerology to obtain your Name Number.

If you choose to do so, you may also use your married name or any other name you have currently adopted if this differs from your given one at birth. You are welcome to experiment with any other name you may have created for yourself or acquired in life to see if the resulting Name Number is more revealing of who you are now. Life is not static, and neither are you!

Here are two examples:

a. J O H N   F I T ZG E R A L D   K E N N E D Y
   1 6 8 5   6 9 2 8 7 5 9 1 3 4   2 5 5 5 5 4 7

b. M A R T I N   L U T H E R   K I N G (omit "Jr.")
   4 1 9 2 9 5   3 3 2 8 5 9   2 9 5 7

2. Add the numbers in each of the names and reduce each to a single digit. Do not reduce any name which comes to either an 11 or a 22.

a.	John	= 20 = 2
	Fitzgerald	= 54 = 9
	Kennedy	= 33 = 6
	2+9+6 = 17 = 8	

President John Fitzgerald Kennedy's Name Number is an 8.

b.	Martin	= 30 = 3
	Luther	= 30 = 3
	King	= 23 = 5
	3+3+5 = 11	

The Reverend Martin Luther King, Jr.'s Name Number is an 11.

NUMBER ONE NAME

Your Number One Name gives people the impression that you are highly individualistic by nature, and you are! You always seem to be dynamically projecting outward your inner thoughts, opinions, and viewpoints. You have an inner conviction in the way you live and don't censor yourself. If there is something that you are doing that you truly like, you do not hesitate to express yourself with the full force of the joy you feel. If you don't like what's going on or some-one in your environment displeases you, you do not hide your irritation or displeasure (although some people would prefer it if you would!).

Your nature is very energetic and you are usually quite enthusiastic about what you do—after all, these are usually *your* plans and projects. You seem to be able to demonstrate your passion for life at any given moment. If other people around you are feeling despondent, you have a way of fueling them and infusing them with your extra energy. In this respect, people look to you as a natural leader. They seek you out for a sense of direction, taking their stimulation from your deep sense of personal conviction. You act as an inspiration for others, as your dynamism is easily contagious.

On the negative side, you may seem self-centered and your personal convictions can make you closed-minded. When people try to talk to you, all you seem to see is your own opinion, without taking into consideration their particular points of view. You can give the impression that you are domineering, even though it may be just yourself over which you have control. Your high energy may come forth in a way that appears too pushy. You may also find that with all good intentions (or not!), people may not wish to go in the direction you are trying to lead them. Your strong sense of personal independence may be interpreted by others as unresponsiveness to the needs of the environment and to the people around you. As a child, you may have been hyperactive, and this may give you a strong sense of impatience as an adult. This quality will often instill a quick temper and volatile disposition.

Famous Number One Names: Mahatma Gandhi, Friedrich Nietzsche, Albert Einstein

NUMBER TWO NAME

Your Number Two Name gives people the impression that you are very sensitive. You generally have a caring disposition and a highly developed sense of feelings. When your friends need someone to talk to, they come to you, as you seem to understand what they are experiencing. Relationships are very important to you, and you seek to build strong and stable connections to the people in your life. Others often consult you when they have problems in their relationships because you seem to have an innate understanding about people, and are likely to know what they are going through and where they are coming from in their lives. As a result, your friends and family look to you for the clarity that arises out of your counseling. You always seem to be there when needed and are perceived as a nurturing person, readily supportive of the circumstances in your immediate environment. Somehow you seem to be a "safety zone" when things are rough, and a focus for security when things are uncertain.

On the negative side, you can be much too sensitive. Every little ripple in the environment can create some type of emotional reaction from you. Even TV commercials could make some individuals with Number Two Names cry. Your emotional nature may move you so much that you frequently change your moods and attitudes. When your sensitivity is not being channeled in positive directions, it can make you rather defensive. When this is carried to an extreme, some people with Number Two Names can be rather reclusive and too sensitive to mingle with most other people. They may also be more secretive than circumstances warrant, making it difficult to communicate in intimate relationships. Sometimes you may feel very emotionally vulnerable, giving the impression that you are needy and clingy. If you are this type of person, you will find that your own need for emotional security can lead to co-dependency and possessiveness in your relationships.

Famous Number Two Names: Ludwig Van Beethoven, Yoko Ono

NUMBER THREE NAME

Your Number Three Name gives other people the impression that you are very communicative and always have something to say about any life situation you encounter. You are generally curious and inquisitive by nature and will investigate any set of circumstances that calls to you. Your innate interest in the world around you and your friendly disposition make you a wonderful person with whom to talk and share life's experiences. People find you mentally stimulating because you know so much about so many things. You are usually very informative and possess a bright intelligence. You like to read and study and usually have an open book or two around. Actually, you are so full of information about everything and everyone that you are very much like a walking book yourself! People love the wide variety of your interests (especially music and the arts). When people spend time around you, they walk away feeling as though their world view has been expanded due to the quantity and variety of issues and ideas you share. In addition, you have a fine sense of humor and a developed wit. You make people think and often make them laugh as well. You like jokes, both telling them and playing them, making you very entertaining and fun to be with. Most people with Number Three Names know how to move freely in social settings, helping others feel at ease and generally spreading comfort in group situations.

On the negative side, many people with Number Three Names talk too much. Other people may feel that they can't seem to get a word in the conversation. Your ideas can be so strong and the amount of information you are giving out so great that you can dominate any social interchange. Yet there are times when it is difficult for you to focus all the information in your mind, and your self-expression may come out confused and flighty. Some Number Three Name individuals can find themselves scattered by all of their information. This is especially the case if they have not developed the proper channels of release for their communicative urges. People may thus perceive them as somewhat superficial and unreliable. The emphasis on mind can create an attitude of emotional detachment and aloofness to such an extent that some people will find you very undependable. You can be so much in your head that you seem unemotional and detached. This can create a certain degree of inconsideration of other people's feelings. Your mind can be moving at such a rapid rate that you appear to be distracted, nervous, and impatient. The solution is finding a way to blend head and heart so that your nature becomes balanced and your demeanor more relaxed.

Famous Number Three Names: Malcolm X, Confucius, Robert Frost

NUMBER FOUR NAME

Your Number Four Name gives others the impression that you are a very practical person. You are usually the type of individual they see going to work every day, paying your bills and taxes on time, taking care of your car, and just being responsible in a very mundane sense. You appear to have your life well organized and under control. People see you as very down to earth—you don't go off into dreamland and fantasize about things that don't matter to you on a day-to-day basis. You seem more interested in buying nice clothes or a new CD than in contemplating deep philosophical issues. You keep your attention firmly set on making money, fixing your attention on the value of the things around you, and using all of your resources to the best of your abilities. You make sure that your own needs and those of your loved ones are taken care of, and you try not to do anything that is unusual or unreasonable. If an idea or decision isn't somehow connected to the way it may affect the outcome of your practical concerns, you let it go, feeling that it is not worth the time and effort of any further consideration.

The more negative side of a Number Four Name may give an individual a strong sense of personal repression. You may find it very difficult to just break loose, break routine, or do something irrational that could turn out to be fun. You may resist taking a chance on having those new experiences that could give you a greater understanding of life. Your need for order in your life has caused you to create so many personal limitations that you don't do what is out of the ordinary, and certainly nothing without a predictable end in sight. Some Number Four Name people are so comfortable with the status quo of their material life that they remain superficially materialistic. They may give the impression to others that they are only thinking about how much their car costs, how good-looking their date is, or how good their grades are without ever noticing the more subtle sides to life. Your inner need is to try to perceive life beyond the mere form of its expression. The quality to develop within yourself is a deeper perception into the *meaning* of life and all events. In this respect, the study of metaphysics, astrology, and numerology may be most helpful for you.

Famous Number Four Names: Peter the Great, Julius Caesar, Napoleon Bonaparte

NUMBER FIVE NAME

Your Number Five Name gives people the impression that you have a very expansive nature. You are refreshingly free of personal repression and limitation and usually ready and eager to try anything new. One of your best qualities is that you see the potential joy in everything that life has to offer. Your accumulation of experiences from all of your adventures gives you an outlook on life that is quite a bit larger than most other people's. In this sense, you may seem like a visionary who is able to see the possibilities that exist in life in ways that are unavailable to most. Your high energy makes you fun to be around, and people generally find you uplifting and stimulating. You enjoy sharing your adventurous nature and may find that you can open up people to a whole world of new potentials. But you certainly don't mind traveling alone. Your ability to make friends is highly developed, and there are always opportunities in your life for new and different kinds of relationships. You are not one to mince words, and your directness cuts right to the heart of the matter. You have an attitude towards life that is very dynamic, which many people respect and admire.

The negative side of a Number Five Name may result in an individual whose sense of personal freedom causes too much of a gap between himself and others. You are so "out there" that others simply cannot relate to you. Your philosophy about life can be so different from the norm that many people may not comprehend how your beliefs can possibly be of help to them. This can cause many disagreements and differences. Your visions and concepts may create the impression in your more pragmatic and materialistic friends that you are a bit "spacey." Most people tend to accept only those ideas and circumstances that affect their immediate lives. Your frame of reference may thus be too "otherworldly," and many people may find that they just can't connect to you. Your sense of personal independence may seem too aloof and detached at times. You can also appear to be nervous and extreme in your actions. Your moods may suddenly shift from jovial to sullen, and there is a distinct need to indulge yourself in pleasure, regardless of the cost.

Famous Number Five Names: Franz Kafka, Mae West, Karl Marx

NUMBER SIX NAME

Your Number Six Name gives others the impression that you are very artistic. Others see you as balanced and beautiful, both in body and mind. You are able to communicate this sense of harmony to the world around you, and are able to see the potential good in everything. You have an innate capacity for developing this beauty into a wide variety of forms of expression. This can be in music, writing, or art, all of which may reflect your natural creative tendencies.

Many people think of you as loving and caring. Your Number Six Name does endow you with an attitude that permits sympathy and compassion in your relationships. Your tolerance of other people is also a fine attribute of the Number Six Name and allows you to accept what other people have to say merely because it is their way of expressing themselves. You are usually quite diplomatic with people, with an innate ability to see all sides of a situation and to come up with a balanced solution that benefits all parties involved. You are very responsible, others feel that they can depend on you, and you are especially present during times of need.

The negative side of a Number Six Name may reveal a nature that is too empathetic and understanding. This may lead to a feeling that other people can walk all over you. Martyrdom went out with the Piscean Age! Yet there are many people with a Number Six Name who tend to be co-dependent in relationships. Your natural ability to connect with people may turn into a suffocating neediness during times of your own emotional weakness. Many Number Six Name people can use all of their energy trying to help others and not use any at all to help themselves. This can lead to a drain on your creative and physical energies. Unless you develop an understanding of and respect for clear emotional boundaries, you will tend to shoulder all the responsibilities for the world and the people around you. Remember, you are 100 percent responsible for 50 percent of each of your relationships!

Famous Number Six Names: Walt Disney, Marcel Marceau, Madame Blavatsky

NUMBER SEVEN NAME

Your Number Seven Name gives others the impression that you are a very analytical person. It's just not logic that you possess, it's something more—a developing sense of intuition. You possess an ability of natural insight that comes from your consistent personal reflection. Your consistent focus upon the inner qualities of life contributes to your strength and depth of character. You have gained much from all the studying you have done. Your contemplation and reflection upon the more subtle currents and patterns of life have developed into a sense of wisdom that other people feel when they are around you. When someone needs an answer to a perplexing issue, they seek you out because you have a piece of good advice for almost everything. At the very least, you offer some wise counsel and a depth of perception into what may bother others. This ability you carry may easily translate into a personal sense of peace. You don't feel threatened by reality because your intuitive attunement allows you to maneuver through even the harshest of circumstances.

The more negative side of a person with a Number Seven Name is the tendency towards being a recluse. Thinking and reflecting so much can cause you to quit experiencing life first-hand. People may thus find you very distant. You can put so much of your attention on your thoughts and contemplations that you may not be open to give of yourself to the people and the environment around you. When you are like this, you may find that you do not hear what other people are saying to you. You lack the ability to concentrate on what is going on around you, as the magnetism of your inner thoughts pulls you so much into yourself. It is then that other people feel that they can't communicate with you.

Sometimes a Number Seven Name gives a distrustful nature. When a person does not reach out to understand others, he or she may become suspicious of other people's motivations. The need here is to develop faith in what other people have to say and not just in your own sense of knowing. When you do not have an immediate answer for a problem in life, you can feel restricted not just by the pressure of that problem but also by your reluctance to consult with anyone else. It then becomes important to open oneself to the help that is always near at hand if we only have eyes to hear and a heart to accept what is being offered to us. Withdrawal into your contemplative state may not always be the correct response to external pressures.

Famous Number Seven Names: Michael de Nostradamus, Isaac Newton, James Joyce

NUMBER EIGHT NAME

Your Number Eight Name gives others the impression that you are a very productive person, and they are right! You know how to create material comfort for yourself. You seek to wear the best clothes, eat the best food, and consume the best drinks. You carry a certain sense of status in your demeanor and seem always to have the money you need for the life situations in which you find yourself. At the very least, you have the ways and means to manifest what is required.

You have a sense of self-confidence that radiates power and control. You take charge, get things done, and are considered dependable by your friends and associates. The majority of people with a Number Eight Name are single-minded and focused. You arrive when you say you will, accomplish what you set out to do, and get done what must be done. The people in your business circle find you an asset to their ventures. You have enough practical insight and enough personal power to manifest your needs and finalize your goals. Your organizational skills are such that you manage to make your life run as smoothly as possible and take pride in your successes.

The negative side of a Number Eight Name is a person with a decidedly materialistic tendency. You may indulge in the glamor of money and power so much that you lose sight of the more subtle personal values that form the basis of friendships and family relationships. You may not take into consideration the effects that your accomplishments have on other people and the environment around you. There is the tendency to judge others for what they have instead of who they are. Some people with a Number Eight Name drive forward towards their goals so intensely that they obtain very little pleasure from their accomplishments. This can make such individuals joyless, sullen, and dry.

If you find that the above is part of your nature, do not be surprised if people are distrustful of your ambitions. You may exhibit so much power that they are afraid you'll walk all over them. You may also be too stubborn and unbending, avoiding other people's opinions and denying their points of view. This would make it hard for people to work with you. (Actually, this kind of a Number Eight Name person would much rather have others work for her!). If right human relationships are not included in one's actions, a person (whether she has a Number Eight Name or any other, for that matter) may end up quite rich but also quite alone.

Famous Number Eight Names: Leonardo Da Vinci, Bette Davis, Groucho Marx, Jean Paul Sartre, Helen Keller

NUMBER NINE NAME

Your Number Nine Name gives others the impression that you are a very compassionate person. They see you as an individual who possesses wide, inclusive views about the human condition. They know that you care about humanity to the point of trying to help in some concrete way. You realize that it takes a great deal of hard work to make even the smallest change in humanity's collective life, yet you are willing to contribute your share. In this respect, we find that many people with a Number Nine Name are very selfless in their ways of giving. Your work and efforts may not create any immediately noticeable results, but you do your best because you believe in what you do. Other people can sense the power of your convictions and be easily inspired by the efforts you project.

You are generally very idealistic. Your Name Number also inspires the romantic and the poet inside you, adding a sense of beauty to the way you express yourself. When people are in a relationship with you, they experience the love you share with them as something very deep and beautifully profound. Your success in life comes not as much from material fulfillment as it does from the development of the refined qualities of your character. It is not hard for you to earn respect and admiration from others.

The negative side of a Number Nine Name may express itself as a tendency towards fanatic idealism. Sometimes the changes you are trying to create turn into a personal battle or thirst for power. It is then that people realize that you are not as giving as you make yourself out to be. Personal integrity and real selflessness are not so easy to maintain. The Number Nine Name person finds that he or she is struggling with sustaining these two subtle but very important qualities of being.

A person can easily lose the power contained in his visions when he is being drained of vital energy. This may happen to a person with a Number Nine Name when he is over-reaching his abilities to help others. Through your Number Nine Name, you may also find that your high idealism can create disappointment when such lofty aspirations are not being fulfilled. In this case, you must watch for depressive states and difficult moods that can cut you off from your own possibilities as well as from help from the people around you.

Famous Number Nine Names: Walt Whitman, Charles Darwin, Marlene Dietrich

NUMBER ELEVEN NAME

Your Number Eleven Name can give others the impression that you are a very spiritually developed person. You can be quite intuitive and psychic and seem to experience life's realities with a penetrating depth and clarity that intrigues people. Quite often, you will find that many people do not really understand you. Yet they know that you have a special perception into some of the mysteries of life, mysteries that are unknown to them. They look to you for insight and may consult you because of your ability to see into life so deeply.

You can be quite an inspiration to the people around you. You don't force anything on others, but just by being who you are, you can reflect certain subtle qualities of your nature that others interpret as a demonstration of your inner strength. When you seek to accomplish something in the world around you, it is fairly certain you will succeed, as you have a definite sense of will power and a clarity of intuition. One of the most important things about the nature of a person with an Eleven Name is that her concerns about life extend far beyond the consideration of her personal life. A person with an Eleven Name is geared for larger, collective issues and finds that she is most comfortable when she is out in the world interacting in as many ways and with as many people as possible. An Eleven Name is out to accomplish a great deal of social change and usually has the communicative abilities to go with such plans and goals.

Since many with a Number Eleven Name are experiencing life in a deeper way, or certainly in a different way, than most others, people may perceive you as eccentric or weird. Your normal level of consciousness is open to receiving a lot more impressions than most people, and this can create a lot of nervous tension. Your super-charged sensitivity may give you the gift of greater awareness but it may also make you quite defensive. This is due to your ability to identify with the slightest "movements" and changes in other people's emotional and mental states.

The more negative side of a person with a Number Eleven Name has to do with a tendency towards impracticality. Such individuals may have a confused and dreamy approach to life. They have little ability to deal with the practical world and with the majority of pragmatic people who inhabit the Earth. They tend to be more inclusive in their philosophical outlook and may find that they are rejected by people whose vision tends to be more personal and limited. Sometimes, the Number Eleven Name person will have a dream that is too utopian in scope to be transformed into a concrete reality. He or she can become trapped in these dreams and accomplish very little of actual worth. Number Eleven Name people may have to learn to go through life without their "rose-colored glasses."

Famous Number Eleven Names: Martin Luther King, Jr., Joseph Pulitzer, Lucille Ball

NUMBER TWENTY-TWO NAME

Your Number Twenty-Two Name gives others the impression that you are an extremely capable individual with an ability to succeed at all you attempt to do. You are also perceived as a person whose scope of vision and area of concern go far beyond the boundaries of purely personal interests. Your frame of reference includes your community, your nation, and extends to the entire world. In this respect, you are usually quite politically astute and globally aware.

You have a highly developed sense of social maturity and are able to be productive in any way you care to express yourself. Although philosophical, you are not a dreamy wonderer. You have the ability to undertake concrete challenges and resolve them practically. Your accomplishments are regarded with respect and admiration, yet the more you do, the more you feel there is to do. Most people with a Number Twenty-Two Name set no limits to their goals and objectives—whatever is conceivable is possible!

The high energy of a person with a Number Twenty-Two Name creates a very charismatic personal projection into the world. People want to be close to you because of the intensity of the life energy you carry. Even when you are quiet and relaxed (which is not a frequent occurrence!), people feel the special excitement a Number Twenty-Two Name person brings into the environment. There are so many people in the world looking for a leader, a teacher, a guide who can take control and tell them what to do and how to do it. You are usually that kind of person, and people look to you for this kind of advice and guidance.

The more negative side to a person with a Number Twenty-Two Name has to do with the abuse of personal power and a misuse of one's talents and abilities. You must watch that you don't use your influence over others for selfish aims and objectives. You have the power to control the direction others take in life and may even have the economic clout to affect the way others live. This strength and authority can be used to satisfy an egocentric urge for achievement and dominance, or you can choose to develop the means to improve the quality of life of the people around you.

The fact of having a Number Twenty-Two Name is not synonymous with either moral courage or spiritual strength. Everyone has to learn eventually how to use his or her life energies for the benefit of the greatest number and to serve the highest good. A person with a Number Twenty-Two Name has the advantage of an abundance of creative potential and, usually, quite a number of developed skills. But this does not necessarily mean that such an individual has obtained either spiritual grace or a sense of personal altruism and generosity. Just because an individual has a Number Twenty-Two Name does not guarantee either financial or moral success. But it certainly contributes to the abundance of the creative possibilities that come your way and which are open to you. You must be very careful not to be motivated by egocentric intentions, as the potency and high energy you usually carry can greatly aid, or if mishandled, greatly harm the people in your immediate circle and beyond.

A Number Twenty-Two Name is very rare. In fact, in my research I came up with only one! Perhaps you can come up with others—if so, please let me know.

Famous Number Twenty-Two Name: Albert Bradley (ex-board chairman of General Motors)

KEYWORDS

Following is a list of keywords and phrases that summarize *how* others see the expression of your basic life urges, drives, and potentials through your Name Number. For example, we could say that the qualities of your nature are projected in a Number One Name through a distinct sense of *yourself*. In a like manner, use the word or phrase written after your particular Name Number:

One	yourself
Two	your relationships
Three	the information you have accumulated
Four	your practical attitudes
Five	your personal freedom
Six	your creativity
Seven	your philosophical beliefs
Eight	your urge for material security
Nine	your ways of helping others
Eleven	your efforts to be of service to your community
Twenty-Two	your ways of aiding humanity and the planet

Your Personality Number

We have seen how your Name Number expresses much of your basic life urges, drives, and potentials. Yet your name—and in this case I am speaking about your full given name at birth—contains even more. Or course, you can work with your married name or any other name change. I just think that in terms of the Personality Number (just as with your entire Name Number), it's a good idea to see "where we came from." If you have had several name changes, we can at least see how such differences in your number vibrations have affected and colored the different stages of your life. If you are contemplating a name change now, you would do well to see how the new modifications in your numbers are likely to affect you in the future.

When we examine the numerological equivalents of the *consonants* in your given name, we can uncover a great deal about the more practica! aspects of your personality. This important area of your life includes your career talents and possibilities as well as the nature of your relationships with friends, family, and other loved ones. The Personality Number describes more of *who* you are to yourself than how others perceive you to be. Naturally, the qualities and characteristics contained in your Name Number may overlap with those found in your Personality Number. This is only natural, for as we shall now discover, the personality dynamics in your life are contained within the numerological vibrations of your name.

There is a total of twenty-six letters in the English language. Of these, five are always considered vowels (A, E, I,

O, U); two letters (Y and W) are sometimes considered vowels and at other times function as consonants.

You should take the letter Y as a vowel when:

1. There are no other vowels within a particular syllable or in the entire name. Y is therefore a vowel in such names as Sibyl, Wynn, Ryan, Lynn, or Lynda.

2. When Y is pronounced like E as in the following names: Mary, Johnny, or Yvonne.

3. When Y follows a true vowel (A, E, I, O, U) and creates one vowel sound. This is called a "diphthong" and appears in such names as Hoyle, Raymond, Reynolds, and Hayes.

At all other times, you should treat Y as a consonant.

W is considered a vowel less frequently than is Y. Nevertheless, you should use W as a vowel in the following cases:

1. When W follows a true vowel and creates the sound of a diphthong. W should be given the value of a vowel in such names as Matthew, Shaw, Shawn, or Lowe.

2. When W follows a D or a G and comes before another vowel. This is the case in such names as Dwight, Gwyn, or Gwendolyn. In these last two cases, both W and Y must be considered as vowels.

HOW TO FIND YOUR PERSONALITY NUMBER

1. Consult the table of letter/number equivalents in the previous chapter to find the numerical value of the *consonants* in your name.

2. Write out your entire name and place the number of each consonant below the corresponding letter. This is how it is done in our two examples:

a. J O H N   F I T Z G E R A L D   K E N N E D Y
   1   85 6   2 87   9   34   2   55 5   4

b. M A R T I N   L U T H E R   K I N G
   4   92 5   3   28 9   2   5 7

3. Add the consonant values in each of the names and reduce to a single digit. Do not reduce any name that comes to either an 11 or a 22.

a. John   = 14 = 5
    Fitzgerald   = 39 = 12 = 3
    Kennedy   = 16 = 7
    5+3+7 = 15 = 6

President John Fitzgerald Kennedy's Personality Number is a 6.

b. Martin   = 20 = 2
    Luther   = 22
    King   = 14 = 5
    2+22+5 = 29 = 11

The Reverend Martin Luther King Jr.'s Personality Number is an 11.

NUMBER ONE PERSONALITY

People who have the Number One as their Personality Number are very aware of their self-identity. They know who they are and why they do what they do. They often feel quite satisfied and confident with themselves as a person. Number One Personalities project themselves into the environment with abundant high energy. They always seem to be doing something. They love athletics and physical activity of any sort, especially if it's competitive. They always seek to have the edge in any contest or game so that they may assert their personal strength over any adversary. They refuse to be overwhelmed or defeated by anyone or anything, be it the other team, or the conditions in which they live.

The Number One Personality is very independent and assertive by nature. If this is your Personality Number, you will be totally ready to overcome any of the odds in life by yourself if necessary. No objective, no oppositional circumstance is too big for you. You are usually quite ambitious and definitely success-oriented. Just given the chance, you will always rise to the top of your chosen profession. Individuals with Number One Personalities have to take care that their assertive nature doesn't become the dominating force in every social situation in which they find themselves. Since they often have more immediate energy than most people, they can tend to push people out of their way in their urge for success.

As children, Number One Personalities tend to be hyperactive. Constantly on the move, adventurous, daring, playful, and mischievous, they can be very hard for parents or teachers to control. Number One Personalities do tend to become more discriminating with their self-projections as they mature. They learn to stay constant in their focus on their objectives and are capable of abundant achievement.

The most important character flaw that can remain a constant in the life of Number One Personalities is self-centeredness. They have lived all of their lives placing so much attention on their need to express their sense of their own identity that they may easily overlook the fact that other people are equally as important. Unless they come face to face with another Number One Personality, they are usually stronger in their self-projection than most other people. The lessons of life will teach them how to look beyond their own viewpoints and the immediacy of their own needs. In this respect, the Number One Personality is learning how to work and cooperate with others, a necessary trait to develop in the Aquarian Age.

NUMBER TWO PERSONALITY

People with a Number Two Personality are very focused on relationships and find themselves continually involved with others. Their developed emotional nature gives them a natural sense of understanding and connection to people and to the environment in which they live, travel, or work. This special sensitivity gives them the ability to develop cooperative conditions so that people can work together to accomplish mutually beneficial plans and projects.

Number Two Personalities understand the intricacies of interpersonal connections and communication. In this respect, they tend to counsel others and help their many friends and acquaintances in reconciling the problems that come up in their relationships. They are supportive of people's growth and life conditions, and frequently find themselves in nurturing positions. They are very reliable when it comes to fulfilling their responsibilities to others. Their sensitivity to the relationship they have to their own environment instills in the Number Two Personality a profound appreciation of beauty, a special fondness for good music, and a love of fine art.

It is a fundamental urge of people with Number Two Personalities to have their emotional needs met through their intimate relationships. If this is not the case, then they may easily become moody and despondent. They have to be careful not to create such closeness artificially, as this can bring about a very co-dependent side to their nature. Number Two Personalities may easily become drained of vitality in their consistent urge to help others and should take care that they have sufficient energy to help and support themselves. An unbalanced Number Two Personality is in constant need of people. In this respect, they may have to learn how to focus on their self-identity while still maintaining their connections with others. They may be so attuned to the feelings of what is going on around them that they become swept away by the emotional charges in their environment. Such circumstances will give Number Two Personalities the opportunities to learn about personal boundaries. If such lessons are not absorbed, Number Twos may find themselves retreating into various forms of escapism and isolation.

NUMBER THREE PERSONALITY

People with a Number Three Personality are decidedly mental by nature and focused on information and communication. They are a storehouse of ideas and thoughts about anything they can get their hands on. The more educated the individual with this Personality Number, the larger is his or her inner encyclopedia of facts, figures, and data. Number Three Personalities are talkative and gregarious. This makes them sociable and usually quite interesting companions. They are clever, witty, and given over to practical jokes. This playful side of their nature makes them fun to be around. They can approach anyone and discuss at length any topic that may come up in conversation. If they don't know anything about the topic (which would be a rarity!), they will sit and listen in order to learn. They are the type of person who in childhood always asks questions. As they grow, they continue to read and study in order to satisfy their innate curiosity. They enjoy writing, sketching, or listening to different types of music, have a wide variety of interests, and can articulate their thoughts clearly, communicating with ease on a broad range of topics.

There is a certain drawback and imbalance to Number Three Personalities when their mental natures are overemphasized. They can then be so mentally polarized that they deny the emotional and feeling nature. So much energy goes into thinking that they neglect the feelings of the people around them. This can make any intimacy with a Number Three Personality rather challenging unless the other person is also predisposed to the mental and rational aspects of life. The Number Three Personality can be hard to reach in a deeper sense and may lack any romantic sensibilities. So unless you are seeking a stimulating mental, platonic relationship, a more emotionally polarized personality can come away feeling rather unsatisfied.

Their active mental nature can also make Number Three Personalities rather nervous. They may have a hard time getting to sleep because their minds are continually on the go. Unless their minds have been able to build the necessary structures for storing and processing all of their information, they may feel scattered and have very short attention spans. One way to balance this tendency is through regular physical workouts combined with aerobic exercise. Another is to cultivate the joy of quiet walks in natural surroundings, as well as taking up one of the arts as a hobby. Physical exercise calms the mind, while nature and the arts stimulate a person's feelings and emotions.

NUMBER FOUR PERSONALITY

The practical affairs of life are very definitely the focus for individuals with Number Four Personalities. Their attention is on how to be responsible and fulfill their practical needs. Career- and success-oriented by nature, these personalities aim to earn enough money to buy the best possible food, clothing, homes, cars, and other material goods and status symbols. It is through the accumulation of these outward symbols of their creativity that Number Four Personalities come to identify themselves and their world.

A cautious lot, Number Four Personalities tend to think things through logically and thoroughly. They are always taking into consideration how their actions are going to affect the physical substance and concerns of their lives. If an action doesn't have some connection to the fulfillment and sustainment of these material needs, it's either unreasonable or nonessential for them. Risk-taking and speculation are definitely not two of their favorite activities! They do not want to do anything which may adversely affect what they have built or are attempting to accumulate.

Number Four Personalities have an established sense of order and structure. They are aware of society's rules and regulations and prefer to follow the accepted way and behave according to the more anchored patterns of life. Productive and responsible, they make it to work on time, do exactly what needs to be done, readily follow orders (or give them), and in general fulfill the demands that are placed upon them or which they create for themselves.

Number Four Personalities are not exactly ebullient. Joyful abandon is just not what they are about! Actually, these personalities can give in to repression and its consequence, depression. They may be very fearful to break with established patterns, following the rules so much that they become stifled and unfulfilled. They can easily imprison themselves by their self-imposed limitations, or by the acceptance of those limitations imposed by society in general. This can give rise to a very strong case of "psychological claustrophobia."

In some cases, Number Four Personalities may have a hard time creating a vision of life other than the way they have stabilized their own lifestyle. It is then that the Number Four Personality becomes stifled, dry, and cold. Such individuals are highly recommended to study metaphysics, as the laws and principles contained within this wisdom can do a great deal to help a person see the relationship between the material plane and the spiritual. Such insights do not deny a person's need for material substance but instead give *meaning* to having and holding.

NUMBER FIVE PERSONALITY

Number Five Personalities are usually upbeat and focused on the expansion of personal experiences. Driven by an inner need for change and growth, they definitely do not want to be tied down to established codes and solidified living conditions. They see the majority of society living in closed boxes on the Earth. Number Five Personalities want to spread their wings and fly—and they do! They are a travel agency's favorite clients, as they travel about in their various adventures here and abroad. They love to experience foreign places, observing different cultures and ways of life. Freedom-loving, they guard their independence. They know that to be tied down would be totally against the nature of their personality. They also enjoy education, taking classes that expand knowledge and, especially, develop new ways of thinking.

If they find themselves in psychological or emotional pain, Number Five Personalities seek out those opportunities that give them the added understanding to cope with and resolve their issues. If what they have experienced truly helps them, they tend to share these experiences with others. Direct and forceful in expressing themselves, when Number Five Personalities believe in something, they state it! Self-censorship is definitely not a facet of this personality type.

If there is anything Number Five Personalities should do to live a more balanced life, it is to work to temper their extreme nature. They can shift between joyful and morose, compassionate and egocentric, with the speed of the jet planes they so much like to fly. They tend towards moodiness and can be quite volatile when they lose their temper. They usually have so much extra energy that if other people or the circumstances in their environment try to restrain them, they may just break through these barriers with explosive force. Number Five Personalities are not known for their practicality, as they spend a great deal of time in the idealism of their visions and aspirations. When this happens they can get caught in a cloud of selfish isolation, wandering off alone into dreamland. Such behavior does nothing to aid in either their own or other people's possibilities for expansion and growth.

NUMBER SIX PERSONALITY

Number Six Personalities are probably the most actively creative and artistic. They have a developed sense of aesthetic taste, a love of beauty, and a definite orientation to refinement. Creativity is fundamental to their nature. They always hold to a vision of how to shape a work of art, the interior design of a room, the presentation of a meal, and all other forms and expressions of life so that they may represent the highest ideals of beauty their talents produce.

Many people possessing a Number Six Personality have the abstract mind of the true artist, even if the arts are not their profession. The sweeping sounds in music create images and patterns in their heads, so much so that the more sensitive of these individuals can be said to "see" the music itself. The subtle meanings in poetry evoke the visions the poet is trying to instill.

It can be definitely stated that Number Six Personalities are the most balanced of all. They certainly have a natural affinity for harmony. They are symmetrical when expressing themselves through the arts, and diplomatic and fair in their relationships. They want to make sure that everyone involved benefits from their participation in life, and they work to improve everyone's surrounding life circumstances by adding their gifts of harmony, beauty, and love. Nice guys!

It is hard to find much that is negative about a Number Six Personality. They love peace too much. They may become overly dependent upon appeasement and co-operation in their relationships. This can lead to a certain tendency towards non-commitment. It is also easy for them to fall into indecisiveness if they do not negotiate an easy avenue of action that benefits all people with whom they are involved. They may also try to escape from their perception of unfairness and the ordinary pains of life. They are idealistic, after all, and their avoidance of the harsher realities of life can and does cause them to become timid and fearful at times. Finally, they have to take care that periodic disillusionment doesn't result in their withdrawal from activities, resulting in lost opportunities to express the beauty that is inside them.

NUMBER SEVEN PERSONALITY

Number Seven Personalities are most focused on the evolution of their minds to enlarge the scope of their communication. They are usually at work developing new theories, original ideas, and advanced forms of their personal expression in order to help the world around them. They are intelligent and analytical, able to think through a situation or condition and come up with interesting solutions. People with Number Seven Personalities enjoy research and study in an effort to understand the challenges of life. They then further these efforts by creating systematic ways of applying these ideas to practical life.

Number Seven Personalities are generally scientifically oriented and have penetrating minds. They cut through the surface layers of any situation to the heart of the matter. They can then organize their ideas most logically, explaining what they see with a new sense of clarity. These people are often in a reflective, contemplative state, trying to tap their greatest potential. Thus they are at work not only in an effort to aid others but also to develop and refine themselves. Their powerful minds allow them to create a vision and transform themselves at the deepest levels. They are therefore always in search of growth. Many Number Seven Personalities are capable of sharing great wisdom as they seek to communicate their perceptions to others and live according to their beliefs.

As with any mentally polarized person, a Number Seven Personality must also be aware of the importance of feelings and emotions. Not everything in life is either a concept or an idea. Since Seven Personalities are primarily motivated by the urge to create a better world, they may be too critical of people and the social environment in which they live. They can easily find faults in everyone and everything around them, not stopping to appreciate that beauty and perfection exist side by side with the need for improvement. They may want to fix things before they are broken! They may also be so self-absorbed that they dissociate from ordinary life and wind up living in an ivory tower. Their challenge has to do with the development of compassion and acceptance as they work to serve the betterment of humanity.

NUMBER EIGHT PERSONALITY

The Number Eight Personality is very involved with creating abundance and material success. People with this personality number are focused on seeing the physical results of their work and efforts. They are very practical and love life's comforts. They strongly appreciate quality—the best clothes, eating at the nicest restaurants, driving the most comfortable cars, and living in the most beautiful houses. They are willing to work hard in order to capture these rewards and are very intense people who know how to get things done. Number Eight Personalities radiate power. They are the natural-born leaders of the world, always drawn to positions of control and influence. It is neither money nor possessions alone that attract the Number Eight Personality. He or she is much more interested in creating those concepts and businesses through which money and success may flow. In this way, not only is success generated on personal levels, but it is also available for others.

As partners or intimates, Eight Personalities exude a certain mysterious quality and may be quite inaccessible at times. Once you have earned their confidence and trust, however, they make the most loyal of friends. Probably the most outstanding personality characteristic of the Number

Eight is a fierce sense of personal independence. These individuals are at their best when they have an area of self-expression that is free from imposed rules and regulations. No wonder they want to be the boss! Number Eight Personalities are generally very self-confident people who are aware of and understand their natural talents and abilities. If they perceive that they are lacking in some area of knowledge or have to develop a quality or characteristic of their personality in order to succeed, they do not hesitate to undertake the necessary education.

Affection and the open demonstration of love can sometimes be a challenge for Number Eight Personalities. Their awareness of the material considerations in life gives them a natural sense of compassion and generosity towards those less fortunate. They can be very active in charity organizations, contributing their time, energy, and money to good causes. Yet on more personal, intimate levels, many Number Eight Personalities can be aloof and emotionally restrained. It is by awakening trust both in others and in the universe that they can learn to realize that closeness to other people does not necessarily have to inhibit their need for independent activity.

The propensity for "the good life" can give a Number Eight Personality a very self-indulgent attitude. This plus his attraction to money and materialism can create a very selfish person. He can become so driven by the rewards of success that he becomes obsessed, never having enough of anything, always seeking more. This leads to a consistent sense of dissatisfaction and may crystallize into anger and depression. The Number Eight Personality has to be open to a very important metaphysical lesson from life—that true material independence and freedom come from an attitude that is not reliant on financial security. The expression "Count your blessings" was probably written for (or by!) a Number Eight Personality.

NUMBER NINE PERSONALITY

People with Number Nine Personalities are humanitarian by nature, seeking to help other men and women through their creative efforts. They are often very selfless people who strive to implement changes in the way people live, contributing in whatever way they can to free people from oppression. This can be on a small scale, such as the work of a psychologist or social worker with a client. Or it can be on a larger scale, such as work with international humanitarian groups like Amnesty International. On whichever level a Number Nine Personality may be operating, his or her work is often accomplished with no great reward other than the satisfaction contained within service.

Number Nine Personalities give freely of themselves and are developing a refined sense of altruism. They are very sensitive to people's living conditions and to the state of our environment. These are highly idealistic people who are definitely at work trying to transform pain and abuse into greater tolerance and understanding. Honest and sincere, Number Nine Personalities also have a keen sense of sympathy and compassion for others. They have to learn that not everyone has such an open attitude, and they may often find themselves disappointed in other people's conduct.

In personal relationships, Nine Personalities are warm and affectionate. They do not have a problem in the creation of intimacy; in fact, their challenge has more to do with correct detachment and objectivity. They are very personal by nature, but sometimes life requires a more impersonal attitude. Number Nine Personalities can become especially attached to their ideals, so much so that when taken to the extreme they may become quite fanatical and narrow-minded. They are capable of very intense emotions, which can, in the defense or advancement of their beliefs and principles, become quite militant or even violent. They may be blind to the forces they are up against and foolhardily throw themselves into some very uncompromising positions. The need for changes in society will always produce people who are against such transformations. The urge for a more universally inclusive world will always be countered by a force for a more limited, exclusive one. Number Nine Personalities do contribute much that is good in the world, but they also have to open up to the realities that exist on a polarized planet like the Earth.

NUMBER ELEVEN PERSONALITY

People with Number Eleven Personalities usually lead very interesting lives. Their main focus is their involvement with spiritual development. This does not necessarily align them with any particular religion, as theirs is a path that can include all faiths. Number Eleven Personalities are less involved with doctrines and theologies and more connected with the underlying, unifying spirit at the core of all true religions and creeds.

These are intuitive and psychic individuals. As such, they are sensitive to the energies of life. We could say that they are "vibrationally aware," meaning that they are more in touch with what *lives* within a person than with what a person may look like. They may be more closely connected to the creative spirit at work through an artist than to the images in his paintings. In essence, Number Eleven

Personalities are having those experiences in life that allow them to recognize and develop *consciousness*. Their ordinary awareness is usually deeper and more penetrating than a person with a lower numerical personality. They can sense the "quality" of other people's thoughts and feelings and are therefore very good at reading people's character.

Psychology and the occult arts (astrology, numerology, and tarot) attract them. If they are professionally engaged in any of these outlets, they often gear their practice to helping others develop spiritually as well. Number Eleven Personalities have a very inclusive point of view about the world. They think much more in wholistic terms and are not judgmental in a way that encourages separatism. The more advanced Eleven Personalities are able to see how everything and everyone is connected within one great web of life, and they believe more in the human family than in any individual nation or culture.

The more difficult and challenging side of an Eleven Personality is the tendency to become rather "spacey" and "out there." These individuals need to develop a practical understanding and build some pragmatic structures to support their wide vision and advanced ideas. The Number Eleven Personality is always at work evolving his or her state of consciousness. Sometimes this work can make such people confused or fearful as they move forward into new areas of awareness. During these times, the Number Eleven person may be plagued by nervous problems and intense physical discomfort. Since they experience the world in a different way than most people, they may seem weird and eccentric, both to others and to themselves. Eventually the Number Eleven Personality will adjust to his or her new state and from this place of expanded vision work to create the avenues from which to share what is being seen.

NUMBER TWENTY-TWO PERSONALITY

As the Number Twenty-Two is considered the "Master Builder," it is only natural that people with this as their personality number focus their lives on big accomplishments. Twenty-Two Personalities are capable of an incredible amount of creative output during their lives. After all, 22 is the double of the highest spiritual power (11) and also contains the practical know-how of the 4. People with Twenty-Two Personalities are extremely high-powered, working out their particular forms of creative self-expression in the most expansive ways possible. Twenty-Two Personalities are often very conscious people who, like Number Elevens, have more energy to share with the world than most. Their lives are often geared to working on large-scale projects that may affect people not only at local levels, but on a national and even a global scale.

Number Twenty-Two Personalities are very charismatic, attracting and magnetizing other people with great ease. These are intense visionaries who know how to bring their ideas out into the practical world. Industrious and responsible, Twenty-Two Personalities are able to work long hours for extended periods of time. They are sincere, no-nonsense types who, just because they are endowed with much, make sure not to waste what they have to give. They work efficiently, embodying the highest forms of leadership abilities, whether at the head of their own group or working as intermediaries in the resolution of conflicts.

The major challenge to people with a Twenty-Two Personality has to do with the right use of will in the administration of the power that often falls into their hands. They must learn the responsibility of handling the influence they have on society. A Master Number does not necessarily indicate a Master. People who have an elevated number (11 or 22) as a major influence in their lives may or may not have the level of spiritual development to handle such tremendous potentials wisely. The same energy that can be used to help others can be perverted by an egocentric person into a force for oppression rather than a vehicle for liberation.

The Twenty-Two Personality who establishes a right attitude towards her responsibilities and talents is a person with unlimited capabilities in her chosen field of endeavor. She can bring power, insight, and an enormous scope of vision into any project or relationship. Her goals are often beyond her personal needs, and as a result she may be emotionally unavailable at times for others. She is occupied with her own inner life and the marshaling of her own abundant internal resources. When the Number Twenty-Two is not living up to her capabilities, she often falls into the lower numerical vibration of the Four, but is even more materialistic! It is then that all the outwardly expansive power of the Twenty-Two is turned to the goals of the little personality. This results in a person who makes great demands on the environment but gives very little of herself in return. This kind of acute shortsightedness coming from such a "large source" eventually leads to alienation and isolation.

KEYWORDS

Following is a list of keywords and phrases that summarize *who* we are in terms of the most important characteristics and traits we find within ourselves. These are the aspects of our nature with which we closely identify in terms of our personality and which are represented by the Personality Number. We could say that the essential quality of my Number One Personality requires me to *be myself*.

Following this example, use the word or phrase written after your own Personality Number.

One	be myself
Two	be receptive to others
Three	be communicative
Four	be practical and dependable
Five	be free to express myself in new ways
Six	be creative in all I do
Seven	expand mentally and philosophically
Eight	create productivity
Nine	be helpful and giving
Eleven	be aware of life's spiritual center in all things
Twenty-Two	be influential in all that I do

Your Soul Urge Number

In the two previous chapters, we examined your outer image and your ways of projecting yourself through the vibration contained in your Name Number, and we looked at your Personality Number and discussed a bit more about your fundamental nature and its characteristics and traits. All of the above are indicative of a person's outer, external nature. Many of us, however, are very hard at work trying to develop our subjective, inner nature. We are seeking a way to contact that intimate, quiet center within each of us. Some call this place of peace (and power!) the contact point to the Soul.

The Soul (or the Higher Self, as it is also known) is alive and well, and rather than it living inside you, you live inside of it. Yet few know the Soul, and fewer can be a conscious and active extension of the Soul's will-to-good. The purpose of all spiritual disciplines, of all spiritual paths, is to bring the personality (the "lower self") in closer contact with the Soul. Most of us identify our lives with our external expression and the images we create around us. We thus become very, very caught up in how we appear to others, our degree of attractiveness, and the need to fulfill all our desires—when we want to and how we want to!

Material possessions and the health and beauty of the physical body are important. After all, we do live on the Earth where the forms of Mother Nature are very powerful. Yet there is a greater, invisible life that becomes increasingly more visible to us as we search for our true purpose and meaning on this planet. This search is one of the main reasons why anyone would pick up and study a book on numerology, astrology, or the tarot. We are looking for (and many of us are finding!) answers to why we are here and where we are going.

The Soul Urge Number is a helpful tool in bringing a clear sense of direction to this search. The Soul Urge speaks to you about your primary inner motivation for growth and development. It is that part of your true nature that is perhaps known only to you and those closest to you. Even then, unless you have been evolving your Soul Urge steadily and consistently, you may only have a glimpse of its possibility and presence in your life. The discovery of your Soul Urge Number and its meaning will make this vital aspect of yourself much more available to you and add power to your life purpose.

HOW TO FIND YOUR SOUL URGE NUMBER

Your Soul Urge Number is found by adding the numerical equivalents of all the *vowels* in your name and reducing them to a single digit or a Master Number. I strongly suggest that you use your full, original given name for this process. Your Soul Urge comes in with you at birth, as does your given name, and remains constant throughout your life. You may wish to experiment, of course. You are welcome to see how the Soul Urge may differ relative to the various names you have adopted, if any, during your life. It is quite possible to manifest and achieve the original Soul Urge under your given name and then have a second Soul purpose reveal itself when and if you have changed your name. I believe, however, that the original Soul Urge vibration as contained in the vowels of your full, given name will maintain a definite influence throughout your life. Certainly secondary influences (through additional names) are possible, especially if you have adopted a name to which you feel a much stronger attachment than you do towards the one you received at birth. This kind of personal discovery is one of the joys and benefits of numerology. So continue to play with the numbers and see what they reveal.

It is very important that you are clear about the use of Y and W when they appear as vowels in your name. Please review what was said about this matter in the previous chapter so that your numerical vowel equivalents are correct.

To find your Soul Urge Number:

1. Write out your entire given name and place the number of each vowel below the corresponding letter. In the examples we have been using, this would appear as follows:

```
a. J O H N    F I T Z G E R A L D    K E N N E D Y
   6            9        5 1            5     5   7

b. M A R T I N      L U T H E R      K I N G
   1     9          3   5            9
```

2. Add the vowels in each of the names and reduce to a single digit (except for 11 and 22).

> a. John   = 6
>   Fitzgerald   = 15 = 6
>   Kennedy   = 17 = 8
>   6+6+8 = 20 = 2
>
> President John Fitzgerald Kennedy's Soul Urge Number is a 2.

b.   Martin   = 10 = 1
       Luther   = 8
       King   = 9
       1+8+9 = 18 = 9

The Reverend Martin Luther King, Jr.'s Soul Urge
Number is a 9.

Please Note: Each of the following Soul Urge Number passages contains a very important spiritual lesson. No matter which of these Numbers relates to you or those close to you, I suggest that you read all of them. You may first wish to read your own; this is only natural. But then go back and study the Soul Urges in order from Number One to Twenty-Two. What you will see unfolding has a great deal to do with the Spiritual Path we all share.

NUMBER ONE SOUL URGE

The Number One Soul Urge is for individualization. Such people are developing a clear sense of who they are and the nature of their personal creative power. They are evolving an inner connection to that loving center within themselves that provides a safe and strong anchor for all of their creative impulses. Their thoughts and ideas contain definitions of who and what they are in ways that distinguish them from other people. It is not that a person with a Number One Soul is striving for separation from others in the outside world. If an individual can function at the level of the soul, he recognizes his inherent connection to everyone and everything.

What is important to a Number One Soul Urge is to "polish his own crystal" so that it may shine as an individual spark of light. Until he can "see" this light within himself, he is a "blind unit" in an ocean of blind units. The awakening of his own conscious stream of light is absolutely essential for further creative and spiritual growth. This stage of awakening is characterized by the Number One Soul Urge. It is often a challenging stage, as it requires a "wake-up call" to life. The loving, creative power contained within the Number One Soul Urge is propelling the individual to be himself, whatever that "self" may mean. This may require breaking free from old patterns that inhibit his progress. Most of the time, such patterns are found within the structure of his relationships with family and intimates. Often it is his mindset or emotional response nature that holds the lock on his growth. Whatever and wherever his "anti-self-creating" habits may be, the life of a Number One Soul Urge person will encounter those circumstances that encourage his individualization process.

NUMBER TWO SOUL URGE

The Number Two Soul Urge deeply instills in people the love of creating connections. Such individuals seek to refine the sense of unity among all people separated by differences in feelings, ideas, or ideals. Their primary motivation in life is inclusivity. Those with a Number Two Soul Urge are very much inclined to create new definitions of relationships that reflect a greater sense of human communality. The goal is a greater sense of cooperation among all individuals so that there is a greater possibility for the circulation of ideas, feelings, and the Life Force itself.

I think it is very important for us to realize that the more we enter through the doors of the New Age, the more crucial it will be for people to embody right human relations as the main theme of life on this planet. The Age of Aquarius is upon us now. Aquarius is the sign of relationships and group endeavor. It is through the development of the individuality in the Number One Soul Urge stage that a person may successfully build the personal relationships symbolized by the Number Two. Once the nature of interpersonal relationships is positively anchored in our consciousness, we are free to pursue more impersonal, group-oriented relationships. This helps us to build those networks of communication that are and will continue to be so important to our contemporary and future lives on Earth.

The Number Two Soul Urge concentrates a person's inner orientation on the "urge to merge." The Number Two Soul is teaching the personality how to connect with others in ways that are mutually beneficial and lead to better group dynamics. The Number Two Soul recognizes that deeper connections among people are only made possible through the feeling nature. In this respect, the Number Two Soul Urge person is inclined to be more emotionally sensitive to people's living conditions as well as to environmental issues in general. When individuals are aware of their Number Two Soul Urge, they recognize that one of the major lessons they are learning is how to feel *nonjudgmentally* what another individual is experiencing and to be supportive in their understanding. This develops intelligent compassion—what a nice gift to receive from life!

NUMBER THREE SOUL URGE

The Number Three Soul Urge is deeply motivated to communicate and express itself. People with this Soul Urge number accomplish this through the tools and talents, information and ideas they have obtained in life. This Soul Urge depends a great deal on intelligence and the mind as its primary source and focus. Individuals with a Number Three Soul Urge are propelled through life with a profound desire to learn and to share what they have discovered through their educational adventures and experiments. They find that the more they grow mentally and the more knowledge they are able to gather, the more vehicles they can create for their inner self-expression.

The Number Three Soul Urge endows a profound friendliness. You want to share what you have learned with others to uplift and enrich their lives. It is important for you to help people see the patterns in life. These are the underlying connections that link others through cultural and language affiliations. You work to enhance these links by adding your ideas and creative impulses to them.

In your outer, working life, your mental capabilities are your strongest point. Through this Soul Urge number, you use mind not in an analytical, separatist way but as a magnetic force to unite and unify. In this respect, you stimulate others to blend their mental talents for the furtherance of group efforts. The Number Three Soul Urge is developing the tools to recognize and describe new visions of life in order that right human relationships may be integrated into daily life.

NUMBER FOUR SOUL URGE

The Number Four Soul Urge teaches us about order. Successful existence on planet Earth requires us to be aware of the practical processes of life. We have to know how to integrate the ideas, desires, and character traits of our personality into the forms and structures of our material life. The Number Four Soul Urge teaches the personality about self-discipline. The inner life motivation is focused on our ability to recognize correct personal and social boundaries and work within them. Thus the Number Four Soul Urge impels the personality to become more fully anchored in the processes of the social structures in which we live. It is through the development of our awareness of the contexts of these structures that we develop the creative power to bring order out of what often appears to be chaos.

The Number Four Soul Urge works on the mind to help shape an individual to be a more productive and contributing part of society. Each of us may then more consciously support the functions of the social system of which we are a part. Since our social system and our life within it are based to a large extent on practical concerns—making money, having a car, keeping a job, taking care of a home— it is through these areas of life that one learns to be responsible to oneself and the environment.

The Number Four Soul Urge encourages the personality to develop positive habit patterns that deal directly with daily occurrences and experiences. By taking part in these patterns, a person recognizes his own and society's limitations and may then learn to transform such limitations into greater freedom.

NUMBER FIVE SOUL URGE

The inner motivation of a Number Five Soul Urge is focused on expansion. The person is encouraged by life to evolve her natural abilities and talents into greater and more varied forms of expression. The Number Five Soul Urge impresses upon the mind the need for freedom of all types and brings this about through experiences in travel, creativity, business, and relationships. Individuals with a Number Five Soul Urge seek the excitement that such opportunities create. Such people are propelled to look beyond the realm of the known and glimpse the possibilities of the unknown. The Number Five Soul Urge endows a person with a powerful imagination. She learns to envision the vague forms of the new possibilities available to her mind and to search out those processes and experiences that can actualize such visions in her daily life.

The Number Five Soul Urge endows an individual with a progressive attitude. Never content with the status quo, such a person seeks to inspire others to go beyond their own preconceived concepts of themselves and open their lives to the realm of greater possibilities. When the soul of a person is truly engaged, that individual is always searching for ways to bring her inner resources to the largest number of people. The soul shares. People with the Number Five Soul Urge share their unbridled enthusiasm for life, their sense of wonder, their courage, and their freedom.

Some numerologists also call the Soul Urge the "Heart's Desire." The Number Five thus brings to the heart the urge to develop many new talents and latent abilities. A person is so moved for change in his life that even if the image of such goals is not fully conceptualized, he will nonetheless go forth on those adventures that can bring such results to him. Such an individual will try any new experience until he knows what it is that he has been searching for. In essence, the Number Five Soul Urge represents the freedom to express one's individual will as the means to greater growth and development.

NUMBER SIX SOUL URGE

The Number Six Soul Urge increases one's motivation to be creative. It thus quickens one's heart to all artistic possibilities.

The mind is impressed with an innate sense of beauty and harmony and is able to perceive deep inside the feelings behind the human experience. In this respect, a person with a Number Six Soul Urge will often use an abstract realm of expression, working with symbols and pictures as her creative tools.

The profound sensitivity that is so much a part of the inner nature of people with a Number Six Soul Urge extends into the environment. Such individuals are always trying to create comfort and emotional support in their surroundings. An aesthetically pleasing environment that stimulates a sense of peace and security is always an appropriate place for the flourishing of the spirit. It provides a setting for harmony and for people to work together in closer cooperation and good will. Many times people are blind to the beauty in their lives. This denial does nothing to improve our life conditions. A Number Six Soul Urge tries to remedy this and bring into our consciousness the more beautiful aspects of life.

The primary goal of a Number Six Soul Urge is the expression of love. It does this creatively through the arts and interpersonally in such intimate settings as the home or workplace. The Number Six Soul Urge also brings the quality of *joy* into life. Happiness is a temporary state, an emotion that is closely connected to the needs and desires of the personality. When such needs and desires are fulfilled, we are happy. When they are denied, we are unhappy. We can be happy or unhappy at twenty different times during a single day—or, if we have a very emotional personality, twenty different times in an hour! But joy is more consistent. It is a quality of our subjective life, and we either have it or we don't. The outer life circumstances matter little to this inner sense of joy. If we are joy-full, we perceive the life around us with all the splendor of it (and our) creative possibilities. Without joy, life has little permanent meaning for us. The Number Six Soul Urge person works to illuminate the life around her with her own internal joy. At the very least, she is engaged in those experiences that seek to touch upon the joyous center of her soul. This is her heart's desire.

NUMBER SEVEN SOUL URGE

The Number Seven Soul Urge indicates a focus on reflection and contemplation. Such individuals are strongly inwardly motivated as they work to develop a deeper understanding of themselves and others. People with a Number Seven Soul Urge try to unlock the mysteries and secrets of life. They want to know how things work, and in this respect they seek to uncover life's causal factors. On a more personal level, this may often extend into a sincere interest in psychology, astrology, numerology, and other fields of study that seek to unlock the inner workings of the human condition.

The Number Seven Soul Urge increases the analytical facets of the mind. Such individuals are being pushed on soul levels towards greater self-development in ways that extend their mental capacities. The urge is to create more intellectual tools that can express deeper and more abstract concepts. This may give rise to an interest in physics, metaphysics, mathematics, and the sciences in general. In addition, another faculty of reason is stimulated—the philosophical. This adds the qualities of inclusivity and broadness to the more analytical orientation described above. A person with a strong Number Seven Soul Urge is often quite happy doing research in a laboratory or library, contemplating the direction humanity is taking, and striving in his or her own way to benefit others. This process tends to lead a person out of the more mundane activities of the outer, ordinary world and into the more subtle workings of inner, subjective reality. Through scientific and/or metaphysical inquiries, such people have the opportunity to develop those theories about life that eventuate into new systems and practices that affect our daily existence.

NUMBER EIGHT SOUL URGE

Unlike the more theoretical Sevens, people with a Number Eight Soul Urge are deeply moved by the process of physical manifestation. Such individuals seek to express their abundant creativity directly on the face of the material world. This Soul Urge has a very healthy orientation. In its most basic application, it can motivate the personality towards greater awareness of and appreciation for the physical body. Care and respect for our physical selves is a very important step towards greater personal and planetary balance and harmony. The Earth is also a "physical body." People with a highly developed Number Eight Soul Urge can stimulate others into taking better care of the environment and supporting ecological causes and projects.

The Number Eight Soul Urge has a vested interest in preserving and improving its own physical organism. It rejoices through and learns a great deal from the five senses! On a broader scale, a beautiful and prosperous planet only gives an individual with a Number Eight Soul Urge a better and wider scope to create the material abundance to which it is so attracted. If the Number Eight Soul Urge is being expressed by a person who is also spiritually developed, this impulse for material supply will extend itself into the lives of others. It is then that such a person becomes the vehicle for helping people financially and creating those products and projects that bring increase and material well-being into the world.

There is an attitude that is all too prevalent in our society. It has to do with an underlying opposition to the acquisition of material things. This creates a great deal of collective confusion, as our society is based on consumerism. What a dilemma! From a moral perspective, the message given out is: "Sensuality is sinful." Yet all around, within and without us, another banner is waved: "Buy, consume, enjoy, be sexy!" Many people with a Number Eight Soul Urge are learning to use their bodies to enjoy their sensuality without becoming obsessed by it. This results in certain life challenges that have as a goal the balance between the physical and non-physical components of our lives.

One of the most profound sayings found in metaphysical teachings is: "The material and the spiritual are the same. The material is the spiritual in physical form. The spiritual is the material in the form of spirit." People who are spiritually advanced and also possess the Number Eight Soul Urge know what this saying means at their innermost core. They are working to teach the truth of this statement through the right use of financial and physical resources and the proper attitude towards our Mother Planet.

NUMBER NINE SOUL URGE

The Number Nine Soul Urge is primarily motivated by the need to stimulate humanitarian efforts. Through Nine, an individual's personality is quickened by this Soul Urge Number to help others and serve society. Whatever the form of one's outer personality expression, be it a

Number Two personality through personal relationships, a Number Three personality through communication, etc., the impulse of this Soul Urge Number is to use one's innate skills to further a cause for the betterment of society or the planet.

The Number Nine Soul Urge is more involved with giving impersonally than receiving anything back. Such people's rewards consist of seeing that their ideals, aspirations, and contributions are being adapted in the world around them. This Soul Urge teaches the lesson of self-sacrifice, a lesson that causes the personality to develop contexts beyond individual desires and the urge for personal gain.

The scope of an individual who is consciously working to live in his or her Number Nine Soul Urge is very inclusive. The challenges in life often involve transformation of personal relationships based in the need to possess or dominate another with the will of one's emotions and the obsession with personal needs. Not so easy! The process is centered on the integration of one's personality orientation for happiness and the soul urge for release from the limitations which our more obsessive personal emotions place upon life.

The Number Nine Soul Urge influences the mind to widen its viewpoints and loosen its control. It opposes a person's insistence that everything in life work out according to his plans and schemes. It opens his inner horizon so that he can see things in broader perspective. The Number Nine Soul Urge often brings a person into contact with relationship situations that call forth his innate goodness and generosity. When this is combined with the kind of mental expansion under the influence of this Soul Urge, a very altruistic individual emerges from the process. This brings about a great sense of release, one caused by breaking through the walls of self-absorption and letting compassion and love flood out into the world.

NUMBER ELEVEN SOUL URGE

People who have a Number Eleven Soul Urge are deeply moved to evolve and express their desire for spiritual perfection. Such individuals are often highly developed in their ability to objectify the nature, quality, and state of what we could call the "Life Force." As we know, everything in the universe is energy. Most people identify with the form side of things, having neither the inclination nor the ability to perceive beyond the form to the more profound reality. This is like dating a person just because he or she *looks* good to us, and being unaware of the inner qualities of that individual. We then wonder after one or two evenings why someone with such a fine appearance turns out to be so incompatible with our need for emotional fulfillment. If we are gifted intuitively, we have the ability to see into the true nature of a person *without projecting either our opinions or our judgments*. We can then relate the form of that person's appearance to the Being who inhabits that body! This type of intuitive insight is often the mark of a spiritually developed person with a Number Eleven Soul Urge.

The faculty of inner sight is open to anyone willing to pursue some form of spiritual discipline on a consistent basis. It is, however, very natural to those with a Number Eleven Soul Urge who experience life much more deeply than most other people and see into various levels of reality. Yet not all people with Number Eleven as their Soul Urge can live up to its spiritual potentials. They may find that an inability to handle their degree of sensitivity makes them very nervous. Their life experiences will teach them to have a more practical approach to their objectives and goals. This is a very idealistic Soul Urge Number, and if mishandled, an individual will have a difficult time perceiving the differences between the possible and the purely imaginary.

One of the primary goals of an individual with a Number Eleven Soul Urge is to enhance his natural psychic and intuitive faculties. Opportunities are sought out in order to develop a spiritual attunement to life. The undertaking of these projects allows for fulfillment of one's "Heart Desire" in the daily life of the personality. People who have a Number Eleven Soul Urge are inspired to move out into the community and use their special sensitivities to help others. They often accomplish this through various forms of consultation and teaching. The challenge to individuals with a Number Eleven Soul Urge is to live up to their inner potentials through the creation of a "field of service" in their outer lives.

NUMBER TWENTY-TWO SOUL URGE

In an earlier chapter, I mentioned that not everyone with a Master Number is a Master. In this respect, it is important not only to speak about the gifts available to the most evolved individuals with a Number Twenty-Two Soul Urge, but also to share some ideas concerning other individuals who find their Soul's Urge expressed through this extraordinary number.

It is hard to imagine anyone with a Number Twenty-Two Soul Urge who is not concerned with large issues. To those who are very egocentric, this powerful energy will make them even more so. They will then try to dominate every social circumstance. As the power of the personality is stronger than the Soul Urge, the energy of the lower self will tend to overpower the more subtle life currents coming from the higher. A necessary crisis will eventuate, forcing the release of one's attachment to whatever fixation or obsession. These crises usually take place in the areas of money and power, or sex and personal relationships. The tendency is for such a person to perceive his or her tiny, personal ego as the center of the universe and make people revolve around its whims, desires, and needs. Such an illusion cannot last for long without precipitating catastrophe. It's that simple!

The majority of people with a Number Twenty-Two Soul Urge have definite humanitarian inclinations. It is important to remember that contained within the 22 is the energy of the 4. Thus, the Number Twenty-Two Soul Urge seeks to express such idealism within the scope of the practical world. Twenty-Two is, after all, the number of the "Master Builder." There is a definite calling to make some significant contribution for the betterment of humanity when Twenty-Two expresses through the Soul Urge. Such individuals can use their profound sensitivities and intelligence to create those forms and structures that may fulfill their lofty purposes. There is always some form of leadership ability in the Twenty-Two. When this drive is focused through the Heart's Desire, the individual is able to fulfill a destiny that transcends mere personal desire.

At the highest level, a spiritually advanced person with a Number Twenty-Two Soul Urge will be motivated in her life directions through the currents and needs of our collective evolution. She will have the skills and personal magnetism to organize and maintain huge projects. Her mind will allow her to influence entire generations with her altruistic thoughts and concepts. Yet this level of Twenty-Two does not and cannot rest on philosophical orientation alone. The forces of consolidation and structure are very important parts of a Twenty-Two Soul Urge's orientation to life. Such a person will have "to bring heaven down to earth" in order to experience that she has done her part in the One Work of World Goodwill.

KEYWORDS

Following is a list of keywords and phrases that summarize *what* inner drive most motivates our lives through the Soul Urge. We could say that the essential quality of my Number One Soul Urge motivates me *towards the expression of the highest qualities of my individuality*. Following this example, use the word or phrase written after your own particular Soul Urge Number.

One	towards the expression of the highest qualities of my individuality
Two	towards the creation of relationships to benefit the greatest number of people
Three	towards the circulation of information that enlightens and uplifts
Four	towards the creation of social structures that sustain society
Five	towards the creation of new experiences that expand consciousness
Six	towards the expression of beauty and harmony that benefits humanity and the planet
Seven	towards research that brings forth new ideas and greater understanding

Eight	towards creating economic opportunities for the benefit of humanity
Nine	towards helping and serving humanity and the planet
Eleven	towards the creation of ways of communication that unite humanity and the planet
Twenty-Two	towards aiding the evolutionary process of humanity and the planet

It All Adds Up!

You now have a working relationship with numerology. The basic information is at your fingertips. To perfect your skills, simply experiment with your own and other people's names and birth dates, and make numerology an active part of your life. Should you wish to expand your insights further, please consult the "Recommended Reading" list at the end of this book.

You may find that there is some overlap among the various elements contained within the Destiny, Name, Personality, and Soul Urge Numbers. This is only natural. Our character, basic nature, personality, and soul freely interchange. There are no firm lines, only fine ones. There are periods in our lives when we are more connected to the image people have of us (Name Number) and adapt it as our own self-image (Personality Number). At other stages, we are closer to the inner motivations of the Soul Urge.

If you have studied astrology, you know that there are three principal signs to a chart. The Sun Sign (telling us a great deal about our vital, creative energy and will power), the Moon Sign (revealing our subjective, emotional nature), and our Rising Sign (the key to our general temperament and projected self-image). The influence of one or another of these signs ebbs and flows, depending on circumstances. It is the same with the various important Numbers discussed in this book.

The key to the success of any life is love. I am speaking here of the power of love, not so much the romantic feelings connected with personal, intimate love. The power of love can be called "the urge to merge." This can easily be directed through the desire nature and the need to possess or be possessed (or both!). We can call this last sentence a description of normal, human, personality-centered love. In this final explanation of the application of numerology to your life, I am speaking about transcendental love, universal love, soul-centered love—there are many names for it. This love is the "quality of consciousness." So the more conscious we are, the more loving we are. Whenever you have a blockage in your consciousness, you have a blockage in your perception of love. Break through the block and you break into love. It's that simple. The occult tools of numerology, astrology, and the tarot help us do just that. They work to raise our consciousness, and as a result, the potential of love in our life. (We also gain an extra skill or two in the learning process—quite a nice bonus!)

When the latent power of love is applied to yourself, you obtain the ability to merge all your pieces into one harmonious unit. You literally "get yourself together." The study of numerology will give you a clearer understanding of your various parts. The following passages summarize the essentials of Chapters 3 through 8. They are presented to make the various parts of your nature as distinct as possible, to help you adapt the numerological system to your view of life.

1. The natural road you travel in life is your *life path*. It is characterized by your *Destiny Number* determined by your *date of birth*. The Destiny Number reveals *where* in life you will most likely work through your Destiny ("karma") and *what* it is that you have to do.

2. You travel along this *life path* through your physical body and its various vehicles. The most obvious of these is seen through your *Name Number* and all of its letter–number equivalents. Your *Name Number*

reveals *how* you are perceived by others and the objective image you present.

3. Within this larger *name* and image, there are two parts. The first is your own subjective image, how you see yourself. This is defined by your *Personality Number*, found by adding the numbers in the *consonants* of your name. The results describe *who* you are to yourself.

4. The second component of your *Name Number* is the *Soul Urge*. This is also called your "Heart's Desire," as it reveals your *inner life motivation* and, from a spiritual point of view, *why* you are here. It is derived by adding the numbers in the *vowels* of your name.

5. We live within cycles of time. One of the most important of these is a nine-year cycle that reveals your *Personal Year*. The number of the Personal Year tells you a great deal about *when* certain life circumstances are due, and by knowing this, you can derive the most benefit from each year's experience.

6. If the *Personal Year Number* is the same as your *Destiny Number*, that particular year is highly significant for you, as it tells *when* a very important set of life circumstances appear. This is your *Success Year Number*. May all your numbers add up to:

```
L  O  V  E  +  J  O Y  +  P  R  O  S  P  E  R  I  T  Y
3  6  4  5  +  1  6 7  +  7  9  6  1  7  5  9  9  2  7
      18 = 9  +  14 = 5  +  62 = 8
            9+5+8 = 22!
```

Other pocket guides from The Crossing Press

Pocket Guide to Ayurvedic Healing
By Candis Cantin Packard
$6.95 • Paper • ISBN 0-89594-764-1

Pocket Guide to Good Food
By Margaret M. Wittenberg
$6.95 • Paper • ISBN 0-89594-747-1

Pocket Herbal Reference Guide
By Debra Nuzzi
$6.95 • Paper • ISBN 0-89594-568-1

Pocket Guide to Aromatherapy
By Kathi Keville
$6.95 • Paper • ISBN 0-89594-815-X

Pocket Guide to Naturopathic Medicine
By Judith Boice
$6.95 • Paper • ISBN 0-89594-821-4

Pocket Guide to Astrology
By Alan Oken
$6.95 • Paper • ISBN 0-89594-820-6

Pocket Guide to the Tarot
By Alan Oken
$6.95 • Paper • 0-89594-822-2

Please look for these books at your local bookstore or order from
The Crossing Press, P.O. Box 1048, Freedom, CA 95019.
Add $2.50 for the first book and 50¢ for each additional book.
Or call toll-free 800-777-1048 with your credit card order.